Instructor's
Teaching Kids to Care

156 activities to help young children cooperate, share, and learn together

Finger plays ● Crafts ● Holiday fun ● Bulletin boards
Send-homes ● Math, science, reading readiness

By Charlene Andolina Trovato,
Preschool Director

To the three men in my life—
Carmen, Nicholas Ross, Carmen Anthony III—
who inspired me with their cooperation and helpfulness
during the writing of this book.

And to Felicia Angelica—
who cooperated by waiting patiently to enter this world.

INSTRUCTOR RESOURCE SERIES

Big Idea Book — 750 best classroom do-its and use-its from Instructor magazine. **IB401.**

Big Basics Book — 55 master plans for teaching the basics, with over 100 reproducibles. **IB402.**

Big Holiday Book — Seasonal songs, stories, poems, plays, and art, plus an activities calendar. **IB403.**

Big Seasonal Arts & Crafts Book — Over 300 projects for special days and seasons. **IB404.**

Big Language Arts Book for Primary Grades — 136 reading and language skills reproducibles. **IB405.**

Big Math Book for Primary Grades — 135 reproducibles on number concepts and processes. **IB406.**

Big Book of Teacher Savers — Class lists, letters to parents, record-keeping forms, calendars, maps, writing forms, and more. **IB407.**

Synonyms, Sentences, and Spelling Bees: Language Skills Book A — 140 reproducibles. **IB408.**

Periods, Paragraphs, and Prepositions: Language Skills Book B — Over 140 reproducibles. **IB409.**

Big Book of Reading Ideas — Teacher-tested reading ideas for use with any reading system. **IB410.**

Teacher's Activity Calendar — Red letter days, ideas, units for the school year. **IB411.**

Early Education Almanac — Hundreds of activities for kindergarten and beyond. **IB412.**

Paper, Pen, and Think — Ideas galore for developing a sequential writing program. **IB413.**

Beating the Bulletin Board Blues — Step-by-step ways to bulletin board learning centers. **IB414.**

Success with Sticky Subjects — Books A and B together offer over 240 reproducible worksheets for classroom drill in problem areas of the curriculum. **Book A—IB415. Book B—IB416.**

Foolproof, Failsafe Seasonal Science — Units, experiments, and quick activities. **IB417.**

Poetry Place Anthology — 605 favorite poems from Instructor, organized for instant access. **IB418.**

Big Book of Plays — 82 original, reproducible plays for all occasions and levels. **IB419.**

Artfully Easy! — "How-to" workshops on teaching art basics, group projects, and more! **IB420.**

Big Book of Study Skills — Techniques and activities for the basic subject areas. **IB421.**

Big Book of Study Skills Reproducibles — Over 125 classroom-tested worksheets for all levels. **IB422.**

Big Book of Computer Activities — A hands-on guide for using computers in every subject. **IB423.**

Read-Aloud Anthology — 98 stories for all grades and all occasions. **IB424.**

Page-a-Day Pursuits — Over 300 reproducibles on famous days, birthdays, and events. **IB425.**

Big Book of Holiday Word Puzzles — 400 skill-builders for 130 year 'round celebrations. **IB426.**

Big Book of Health and Safety — Reproducible activities to shape up the health curriculum. **IB427.**

Teacher Savers Two — Reproducible awards, contracts, letters, sanity-keepers galore. **IB428.**

Celebrate America — Over 200 reproducible activities about the symbols, the land, the people of the U.S.A. Maps, graphs, timelines, folklore, and more. Eight pull-out posters. **IB429.**

Big Book of Absolutely Everything — 1001 ideas to take you through the school year. **IB430.**

Language Unlimited — 160 reproducibles sharpen reading, writing, speaking, listening skills. **IB431.**

Children and Media — Activities help kids learn from TV, radio, film, videotape, print. **IB432.**

Blockbuster Bulletin Boards — 366 teacher originals for all grades, subjects, and seasons. **IB433.**

Hey Gang! Let's Put On A Show — 50 original skits, choral readings, plays for all ages. **IB434.**

Puzzle Pals — Mazes, decoders, wordsearches, hidden objects and more. **IB435.**

Hands-On Science — Jam-packed with facts and activities to develop young scientists, K-8. **IB436.**

21st Century Discipline — Practical strategies to teach students responsibility and self-control. **IB437.**

Learning to Teach — A blend of research on teaching with the practical insights of experienced teachers. **IB438.**

Loving Literature — Literature selections and accompanying activities that encourage kids to laugh, cry, wonder, and keep on reading. **IB439.**

Teaching Kids to Care — 156 activities to help young children cooperate, share, and learn together. **IB250.**

Games, Giggles, and Giant Steps - 250 games for children ages 2-8; no equipment needed. **IB251**

Everybody Sing and Dance - 80 hands-on, shoes-off song, dance, rhythm, and creative movement experiences. **IB252**

Author, Charlene Andolino Trovato; Editor, Nancy Jo Hereford; Designer, Amelia Bellows; Illustrator, Patty Briles; Copy Editors, Susan Gaustad and Anne Rickards. Cover photograph by David Grossman. The Instructor Books staff: Judy Cohn, Director; Jane Schall, Executive Editor; Diane Bello Peragine, Editor; Vanessa Byrd, Andrea Junker, and Jeanne Johnson, Production Coordinators.

CONTENTS

Teaching today's kids to care!

CONTINUED

I t is the first day of school and the children and parents enter your schoolroom. You observe that some children immediately begin to play with other children. Another group of children races into the room, grabs toys, pushes, and is generally disruptive. A few children stand back and watch the activity. A couple of children linger by the door, clinging to their mothers, worrying about the inevitable separation.

Whether the children in your class are outgoing, aggressive, timid, or frightened, each one has specific needs. One crucial common need of all young children is the need to learn prosocial behavior—that is, getting along with others, developing positive friendships, and becoming part of the group. The development of these behaviors cannot be left to chance. They need to be formally and informally taught and nurtured in a supportive classroom setting throughout the day. Teachers are responsible for providing numerous and varied opportunities for their students to learn and practice prosocial behavior.

Teaching these behaviors is a difficult and demanding job for early childhood educators. It requires understanding, loving, and knowledgeable teachers: teachers who can meet the needs of a variety of children; teachers who are aware of current research trends, are organized, have planned prosocial activities, and who themselves model prosocial behavior.

Children who begin to develop prosocial behavior at an early age feel good about themselves as people. They acquire a positive self-image and high self-esteem. Daily life and challenges of school become easier and more rewarding. New situations and people are approached with confidence.

CONTINUED

It is our hope that this book will help teachers, care givers, and parents of children ages two through six understand, nurture, and teach prosocial skills in a healthy classroom environment.

● **Part I, "Getting Ready to Teach Prosocial Behavior,"** begins with a short Teacher Quiz to help you as a teacher assess your current knowledge of this area. The next section of the chapter provides specific research facts and definitions. The remainder of the chapter focuses on indirect methods of teaching prosocial behavior—enhancing and promoting a prosocial environment.

● **Part II, "Prosocial Fun for Everyone,"** is filled with original, creative activities to directly teach and reinforce prosocial skills in all areas of the early childhood curriculum.

● **Part III, "Parents as Partners in Prosocial Development,"** features a variety of original reproducible send-home activities to involve parents in the development of prosocial behavior in their children.

● **Parts IV and V, "Friends with Special Needs"** and **"Friends Around the World"** contain reproducible activities to help your students develop a sensitivity to children from different cultures and children with special needs.

● **"Prosocial Resources"** lists professional publications to expand your awareness of the development of prosocial behavior.

Getting ready to teach prosocial behavior

T he study of prosocial behavior of young children is relatively new, beginning around the late 1970s. Teaching it will be easier if you have an understanding of what has been learned about the development and instruction of prosocial behavior. Without an adequate base of knowledge, many daily incidental teaching opportunities could be lost.

Part I is designed to give you a brief overview of the latest research and current trends. It begins with a short ten-question multiple choice quiz to help you gauge your current level of knowledge on the subject. Don't be discouraged if you're not familiar with the information. Remember, it is a new area and the purpose of this book is to help you learn to teach prosocial behavior formally and informally. In this section, you will discover the definition of prosocial behavior, what recent research has reported, and how to create a prosocial classroom environment. Your goal is to find the answers to the quiz questions as you read. At the end of Part I, you will have a good knowledge of a new and growing area of the ECE curriculum—the development of prosocial behavior.

The Prosocial Pop Quiz:

Ten Practical Questions to Ask Myself about Prosocial Behaviors

DIRECTIONS

● Read the questions and circle your answer or answers. (There may be more than one answer for a question.)

● Check your answers with the correct ones at the bottom of the following page.

● Read Chapter 1 and learn about prosocial behavior!

1. **What is the definition of prosocial behavior?**
A. The way children behave in a structured environment
B. What children do to assist other children without expecting a verbal or nonverbal reward

2. **What specific behaviors come under the heading of prosocial behavior?**
A. Cooperation   C. Helping
B. Aggression   D. Assertiveness

3. **According to research, is prosocial behavior learned or the result of maturation?**
A. Learned   C. Both A and B
B. Maturation

4. **What are three important personal and professional qualities for a teacher who facilitates prosocial behavior?**
A. Disciplinarian   C. Understanding
B. Loving   D. Knowledgeable

5. **What does the broad term "environment" mean in an early childhood setting?**
A. The way your classroom has been arranged
B. The physical arrangement of the room and the personal and professional characteristics of the teacher or care giver

6. **How does the physical arrangement of the classroom contribute to the children's interactions with each other?**
A. Attractive, orderly rooms invite children to enter and freely explore the surroundings.
B. Attractive, orderly rooms invite children to do what they want to do.

7. **What are two methods of teaching prosocial behavior?**
A. Direct   C. Structured
B. Indirect

8. **What are two key factors that contribute to an increase in prosocial behavior with age?**
A. Level of cognitive development   C. Number of playmates
B. Environment

9. **Why is a daily classroom schedule important for the development of prosocial behavior?**
A. It provides time for both planned and spontaneous teaching.
B. It allows teachers to change the routine daily.

10. **What activity centers tend to foster prosocial behavior?**
A. Block center   C. Library   E. A, B, C, & D
B. Time-out area   D. Manipulatives   F. A, C, & D

ANSWERS: 1-B; 2-A and C; 3-C; 4-B, C, and D; 5-B; 6-A; 7-A and B; 8-A and B; 9-A; 10-E

WHAT ARE PROSOCIAL SKILLS?

'Prosocial behavior is a child's actions to aid or benefit another child or group of children without considering the possibility of an external reward.'

What are the specific actions that can be observed that would aid or benefit another child? These actions, referred to as prosocial behaviors, fall into two broad categories: **cooperating** and **helping.**

COOPERATING is the ability of two children to play or work toward a common goal in a variety of situations. Cooperating is seen, for example, when a group of children works together to move the gym equipment to one side of the room so that you can set up the record player for an aerobics workout. During play time a group of children cooperates when each chooses a block to build a rocket ship.

HELPING behavior is comprised of four behaviors: rescuing, defending, sharing (materials and information), and comforting.

● **RESCUING** behavior occurs when one child sees another child walk toward a moving swing and pushes him or her to safety.

● **DEFENDING** behavior is observed when one child verbally sticks up for another child

in an honest, positive way. When Susan accuses Patty of spilling sand on the floor, John explains that it was there before Patty came to school.

● **SHARING MATERIALS** is the most common prosocial behavior exhibited by young children. Joan needs a cup of water for her finger painting. Peter places his cup of water between them so they can both use it.

● **COMFORTING** activities occur mainly through verbal communication skills. When, for example, Leslie begins to cry for her mother, Jan puts her arm around Leslie's shoulder and explains that all mothers will be coming soon.

All six of the prosocial behaviors are equally important for young children to learn. When an entire class learns to cooperate with each other and acts in helpful ways, everyone benefits. The classroom becomes a happy, friendly, relaxing place to work and play. Everyone joins together to quickly accomplish the daily routine.

Research facts

Research on the development and enhancement of prosocial behavior began around the late 1970s. Prior to that time, researchers focused on the behaviors that resulted from the absence of adaptive prosocial behavior: aggression and emotional disturbance. Recently, prosocial behavior has actually been referred to as an alternative to aggression. Just as children learn to act out by hitting, punching, pulling, grabbing, and name-calling, they can also learn to act positively or prosocially during the early years.

It is encouraging that this topic, so important to the well-being of society, is finally receiving attention from researchers and practitioners. Here are the most important research questions and answers on prosocial behavior.

Q & A

Q **At what age is a child capable of exhibiting prosocial behavior?**

A According to Freudian or developmental theorists, children are not capable of concern for others until about the age of five or six. Before that age, children are only interested in their needs with little regard for others.

Piagetian or cognitive developmental theorists agree that young children have a very difficult time exhibiting concern for others.

Moral development researchers also report that children with mature moral judgment exhibit more helping and generosity behaviors than children at a lower level of moral reasoning.

Q **Do children become more prosocial with age?**

A Researchers found no relationship between age and prosocial behavior before the age of 4. However, the relationship increased positively for children from 4 to 11. Many researchers have supported this positive relationship between age and prosocial behaviors.

Q What key factors contribute to an increase in prosocial behavior with age?

A The major factor contributing to an increase in prosocial behavior appears to be a higher level of cognitive development. In most children, prosocial behavior increases with advanced mental capacity. However, cognitive development alone cannot be considered sufficient to increase prosocial behavior. Environmental influences have also been reported as determinants of increased prosocial behavior.

Children who observe prosocial behaviors from their parents and teachers are more likely to develop those behaviors than children who do not have good home and school models, even if the children are at the same level of cognitive development.

Q Is prosocial behavior learned, or does it result from maturation?

A Research clearly shows that maturation is essential to development of prosocial behavior. However, maturation alone does not guarantee the development of these behaviors.

Prosocial behavior needs to be taught, modeled, and nurtured in the home and school. Parents, care givers, and teachers need to know how these behaviors develop and to nurture them in a supportive environment.

Q How can prosocial behavior be taught?

A Prosocial behavior can be taught either indirectly or directly.

During direct teaching, the teacher tells, then demonstrates the behaviors through a variety of planned creative activities and experiences.

Three indirect ways of teaching prosocial behavior are modeling, rewarding, and planning. Teachers model prosocial behavior as they interact with children throughout the day. In rewarding, teachers present verbal or nonverbal positive reinforcement to encourage children to exhibit appropriate behaviors more frequently. Teachers plan the environment to enhance positive interactions among the children during their daily routine.

An ECE program that teaches and nurtures prosocial behavior incorporates both direct and indirect strategies.

CREATING A PROSOCIAL ENVIRONMENT

Planning and arranging a prosocial environment is the first step toward creating an atmosphere where children can work and play in harmony. A healthy environment promotes and enhances the development of a positive self-concept and self-image in young children.

Two environmental factors work together to facilitate prosocial behavior in an early childhood setting: (1) interested, accepting, communicative teachers, and (2) an attractive,

orderly, cheerful classroom. An adequate prosocial environment, therefore, is a combination of personal qualities—teacher, care giver, aide—and physical qualities.

In the classroom, the teacher makes the difference. On the one hand, the teacher is responsible for exhibiting personal traits that foster prosocial development. On the other hand, the teacher is responsible for creating and planning a classroom designed to stimulate prosocial behavior.

PERSONAL QUALITIES

Creating a Climate:

- **Setting the Tone**

- **Knowing Each Child**

PHYSICAL QUALITIES

Creating an Environment:

- **Room Arrangement**

- **Materials and Equipment**

- **Daily Schedule**

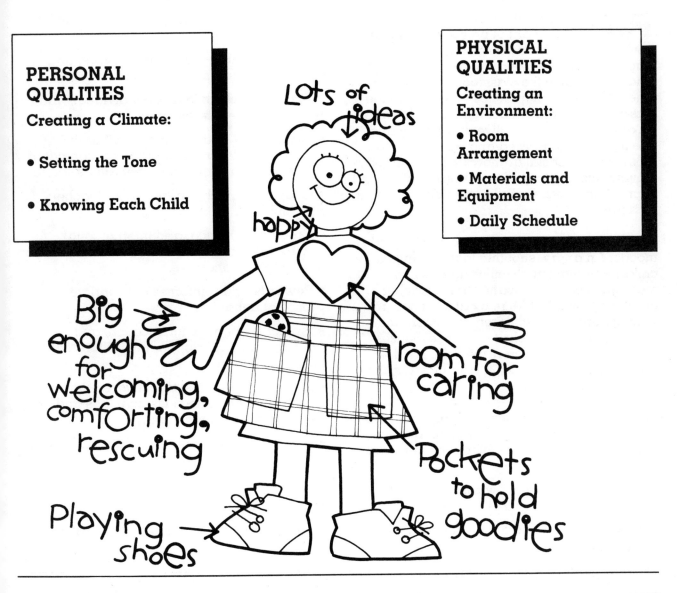

HOW YOU CREATE THE CLIMATE

Two teacher practices determine whether a child will learn and exhibit prosocial behavior. These practices are modeling and reinforcing the prosocial behaviors of cooperation and helpfulness.

MODELING PROSOCIAL BEHAVIOR

Modeling is the most powerful determinant of prosocial behavior. Directly and indirectly, you, the teacher, care giver, or aide, control much of what happens in the classroom. You set the tone. The personal qualities you bring to the classroom make a critical difference between an atmosphere that is alive and happy and one that is disorganized and apathetic. You create the prosocial framework by your body movements, the tone of your voice, your facial expressions, your verbal comments, and your gestures.

Children are sensitive to your attitudes and moods. An angry, shouting teacher invites children to react in a similar aggressive manner. A calm, pleasant, strong teacher creates a comfortable, relaxed, and secure atmosphere where children can learn and grow. Adult models elicit similar responses from youngsters. If you respect the children and their needs and act in helpful ways, they will respond in kind.

The following list of teacher actions will help you become aware of other human qualities that inspire prosocial development in young children.

• Greets children with a warm smile and friendly comment.

• Presents a calm and gentle manner, and is altruistic and empathetic.

• Exhibits a sense of humor.

• Feels good about himself or herself and his or her job.

• Makes children feel welcome, safe, and secure, and gains their respect.

• Accepts each child as an individual, and has a genuine interest in each.

• Plans direct and indirect activities to facilitate the learning of prosocial behaviors while demonstrating these behaviors.

• Cooperates with parents, other teachers, and children.

• Creates a physical and interpersonal environment designed to develop cooperation and helping behaviors.

• Rewards and reinforces appropriate prosocial behavior.

• Promotes open communication, and provides numerous opportunities for young children to share.

• Encourages at least two children to work together to complete classroom jobs and helps kids interact at lunch or play.

• Helps each child find his or her place in the group.

• Comforts children when necessary.

• Rescues children from danger.

• Is dedicated to the total education of young children.

REINFORCING AND REWARDING

Prosocial behaviors are learned behaviors. When learned behaviors are followed by a reward, they are likely to occur again; therefore, rewarding cooperation and helpfulness increases their occurrence.

Several types of rewards are verbal praise, activities and privileges, and nonverbal approval. Every child responds to one or more of these rewards.

Verbal praise is the most common and effective type of reward in an ECE classroom. Thanking a child for cleaning up so quickly or helping a new child find the scissors lets him or her know that you approve of the action.

Activities and privileges are also effective methods of rewarding desired behaviors. When, for example, John gets to be line leader after sharing his special toy with Susan, he is suddenly eager to share with the other children.

Two of the most common types of nonverbal reinforcement are physical contact and tokens. Physical contact, such as a pat on the head, acknowledges a child's helpful or cooperative behavior. This is a good method for a shy child who does not like to draw attention to himself or herself.

Tokens, such as buttons with smiling faces, stickers, stars, or checks placed on a chart of cooperative or helpful behavior, increase those behaviors. Rewards of this kind given to a group rather than to individuals are consistently more effective. Competition among the group members decreases, and the children are friendlier as they work toward common goals.

Many teachers have found that the following are appropriate reinforcers for most young children.

VERBAL APPROVAL

GOOD	GREAT	CORRECT	EXCELLENT
Good thinking.	I like that.	You did a nice job.	I like the
Good building together.	Nice cleaning up.	This group worked hard.	way you share.

ACTIVITIES AND PRIVILEGES

Going to the playground	Selecting a story to read	Being a line leader
Feeding the animals	Passing out objects	Having the job of door holder
Helping the teacher	Choosing an activity on his or her own	

NONVERBAL COMMUNICATION

Smiling	Grinning	Touching the shoulder
Clapping hands	Laughing	Winking
Hugging	Tousling hair	

TOKENS/CHARTS

Stars	Checks	Stickers	Smiling faces	Hearts

KNOW EACH CHILD

A teacher's first contact with a young child is generally through the information obtained from a student information form. Usually, the form is sent to the parents and returned to the teacher before the first day of school. A good teacher reads this information carefully and uses it wisely.

A brief comment to each child on the first day of school about a pet, sibling, or grandparent sets a warm, inviting, friendly tone. Background information also helps you understand a little about a child's current prosocial behaviors. If, for example, John is an only child, he may have difficulty sharing. Or Jan may cry for her mother during the morning since they have never been separated. A recent divorce may cause Patty to be angry and hurtful.

Knowing each child makes your job easier. Send the following reproducible form along with the other enrollment forms your school may have. Keep all of them handy for easy reference. It will give you a great deal of insight into your students' behavior.

Tell us about your child

Special attachments _____

Likes _____

Dislikes _____

Toileting names _____

Habits _____

Particular fears _____

How is child's anger expressed? _____

How do you discipline your child? _____

Has your child ever been separated from you? _____

How did he or she handle it? _____

Has your child ever been hospitalized? _____

Child's strengths, in your opinion _____

Any additional information about your child: _____

_____

_____

_____

Health insurance coverage _____

Any special medical problems? _____

_____

_____

_____

_____

_____   _____
Parent's Signature   Date

TEACHING KIDS TO CARE **17**

HOW YOUR ROOM CREATES THE CLIMATE

The physical appearance of your classroom has a great deal to do with the development of prosocial behavior. A colorful, attractive, orderly room invites the children to enter and freely explore everything in their view. The furniture and equipment should be scaled to the height of the children. The material should be at eye level and neatly arranged on shelves in individual containers.

The physical arrangement of the classroom has a profound effect on prosocial interaction among children. It should offer a variety of activity centers and materials that encourage and enhance spontaneous interactions among several children at one time.

It is helpful if your room contains some or all—depending on budget and space limitations—of the following activity centers, materials, and equipment.

● **BLOCKS.** The block area should be spacious and well equipped. This tells the children that there is room for more than one child at a time to build and construct. In addition to the different sized blocks, it is beneficial to have small cars and trucks, road signs, miniature people, tools, and perhaps a manipulative train arranged on shelves surrounding the building space. This often leads to a large group building project or several small projects where the children share comments about their work.

● **LIBRARY CENTER.** Visit your local or school library to obtain as many books as possible that encourage prosocial behavior. (See the activities section of this book for a list of appropriate children's literature.) It is nice to have a quiet corner with a sofa, comfortable cushions, pillows, or carpet pieces. Several children can enjoy listening to tapes as they relax.

● **MANIPULATIVE AREA.** Cabinets should surround tables with containers of Legos, table and floor puzzles of increasing difficulty, parquetry blocks, peg boards, sequencing cards, memory games, matching cards, and more. These types of materials encourage small groups of two or three children to work together to complete a task.

● **ART.** At the art table, surrounded by cabinets filled with paper, glue, crayons, magic markers, Play-doh, cookie cutters, stencils, paper scraps, glitter, watercolors, and paints, the children learn to share the materials and talk about their creations. At the easels the children help one another put on smocks and share their paint cups.

● **PUPPET STAGE.** The puppet stage with chairs in a semicircle in the front for a small audience and room behind for enough children to work several puppets is a wonderful place for children to cooperate. The children decide which puppets they are going to use, then they work together to put on a show for their audience.

● PLAYHOUSE OR DRAMATIC PLAY AREA.
More opportunities to develop prosocial behavior will occur in this area than any other. The children come together in a familiar situation such as daily family life. This interesting center needs to provide a variety of dress-up clothes, a long mirror, kitchen equipment and utensils, table and chairs, high chair, crib, dolls, pillows, and a house front with windows and functioning door. The children cooperate and help one another as they pretend to cook meals, set the table, feed and diaper the baby, dress for work. You can immediately observe which kids are exposed to prosocial behaviors at home.

● INDOOR GYM AREA. On the jungle gym, the children learn to take turns climbing and swinging, share riding toys, and cooperate during game-playing. The children work side by side at the sandbox building roads, mountains, tunnels, and rivers as they informally talk with each other.

● MUSIC AREA. A small group area with a variety of records, tapes, and musical instruments brings children together to sing, dance, march, and tap out beats to the music. In this center, children listen to and follow the directions on the records or tapes. They join together for warm-up exercises of running, walking, and jogging.

● SCIENCE DISCOVERY AREA. This center should be rich with science manipulatives. Several magnets with assorted objects in containers, measuring cups and small beads, scales and weights, magnifying glasses and a microscope with slides are natural materials to encourage children to cooperate and help each other while discovering the wonders of science.

● GROUP AREA. This is the center where the day begins with a look at the calendar, opening songs, a time for sharing, planning and discussing the day's activities. Later in the day this area is for storytelling, and creative dramatics. The children feel a part of the group, planning and working together to meet common daily goals.

● THE OUTDOOR ENVIRONMENT. The outdoor equipment needs to be arranged to enhance group play. A small area can be roped off to plant a garden. The children can be responsible for daily watering and care. Children can also be given paint brushes and buckets of water to "paint" the side of the building. Other children can participate in a teacher-organized relay race.

Outdoor gross motor equipment stimulates the development of prosocial behaviors. Large furniture boxes enable several children to make hideouts, tents, rocketships, and more.

All activity centers, when well equipped, organized, and attractive, indirectly nurture prosocial development. Many times throughout the day the children will experience spontaneous situations that require them to practice cooperation and helping behaviors.

CONTINUED

A PROSOCIAL SETTING CHECKLIST

Once a month during a staff meeting, it is helpful to evaluate your prosocial physical environment. The room arrangement, materials, and equipment may or may not be currently meeting your prosocial goals. Does, for example, the block area need to be enlarged to adequately handle the number of interested children? Do you have enough of the most popular dress-up clothes to stimulate dramatic play? Are the floor puzzles challenging enough to encourage children to work together in this problem-solving situation?

Here is a handy little checklist to help keep your environment on target throughout the year.

	YES	NO
1. Is the room clean, comfortable, and pleasant?	___	___
2. Does each activity center have enough room for children to move around freely?	___	___
3. Are the teachers adequately interacting with the children?	___	___
4. Are the equipment and materials appropriate for the age and interest of the children?	___	___
5. Do the equipment and materials encourage cooperative behavior?	___	___
6. Are there adequate materials for sharing?	___	___
7. Are the activity centers arranged to facilitate interactions between children?	___	___
8. Is there adequate space for both noisy and quiet activities?	___	___
9. Are the activity centers clearly defined to avoid confusion?	___	___
10. Does the daily schedule allow adequate time for children to become involved in an activity?	___	___

	YES	NO
11. Are the activity centers surrounded by materials that:		
● lead to dramatic play?	___	___
● provide for physical activity?	___	___
● require manipulation of materials?	___	___
● encourage construction?	___	___
● inspire creative expression?	___	___
● demand communication of ideas?	___	___
● encourage sharing, cooperation, and helpfulness?	___	___
12. is the room bright and cheery?	___	___
13. Are the bulletin board displays changed often, and do they reflect an appropriate theme?	___	___
14. Are broken toys, puzzles with lost pieces, and damaged materials replaced?	___	___

SCHEDULING FOR PROSOCIAL BEHAVIOR

A day in an early childhood classroom is always hectic and busy. Children paint, listen to stories, have snacks, participate in music and movement activities, and more. But—is there enough time for both planned and spontaneous activities through the day?

A well-planned daily schedule provides the time children need during the day to get involved in group play and work. The schedule provides a routine for the day which makes young children feel safe and secure. They know what to expect. Their day has order. Most important, a daily schedule creates a smooth flow from one activity to another. This flow gives children time and teaches them to interact in a variety of learning and play situations.

The daily schedule is as personal to each program as the physical design. It is, however, important that each program has a routine that includes time for:

● Greeting children and parents

● Free play, indoor and outdoor

● Small group time:

Morning exercises

Music

Art

Cognitive development

Large motor development

Stories, finger plays, creative dramatics, puppetry

● Cleanup

● Transition times

● Daily breaks—bathroom, snack, rest, lunch

● Individually chosen activities

● Dismissal:

Organizing art work and lunch boxes

Putting on coats

Saying good-bye

PART II

Prosocial fun for everyone

Young children two, three, four, five, and six years old thrive when their learning activities are creative, fun, easy-to-do, and stretch the imagination. This chapter is packed with reproducible, fun-to-do activities to help your youngsters develop cooperation and helping behaviors. You'll find exciting ideas to encourage children to work and play together in a friendly, happy atmosphere. Featured in this chapter are songs, finger plays, cooking experiences, reading and math readiness projects, large motor development activities, arts and crafts, bulletin board ideas, puppetry, holiday fun, and more—all designed to help you promote prosocial behavior. In addition, patterns and sample illustrations have been included to lessen teacher preparation time.

Working together for reading readiness

Many prosocial behaviors can be taught and reinforced while getting children ready for reading. Children will love to work together on projects designed to teach letters and sounds of the alphabet, word recognition, and matching. In this section, you'll also find ideas for group language experience stories to increase oral language and basic skill development while encouraging helping and cooperating behaviors.

ACTIVITY

The name game

BEHAVIOR: Helping

ACTIVITY: Recognition game

MATERIALS: paper strips with the name of each child in the group marker

DIRECTIONS:

1. Place the name strips around the room first thing in the morning.

2. Ask the children to look for the names at a transition time.

3. Children find a name and give it to the correct child.

4. Kids must find all names before the next activity begins.

Just use 1st letter
for all kids

The letter people

BEHAVIORS: Cooperating, sharing (materials and information)

ACTIVITY: Language arts and reading readiness

MATERIALS: letters A-Z (each on separate pieces of paper for posters)

markers

2 names beginning with each letter

5 or more pictures of objects for each letter

glue

DIRECTIONS: **1.** Begin with the letter "A" and work through the alphabet. Take your time; the process should take several months with young children.

2. Tell the kids two possible names that begin, for example, with the letter "A." You could suggest Allen or Albert.

3. Have children vote on the name that they would like to use.

4. Glue the name to the letter person poster. Place five pictures beginning with that letter sound on the board, and let children vote on two pictures they would like the letter person to have.

5. Glue the objects to the poster.

After each picture is complete, display it in the classroom for all to see. Pictures look great suspended from the ceiling.

—Beatrice Eaton

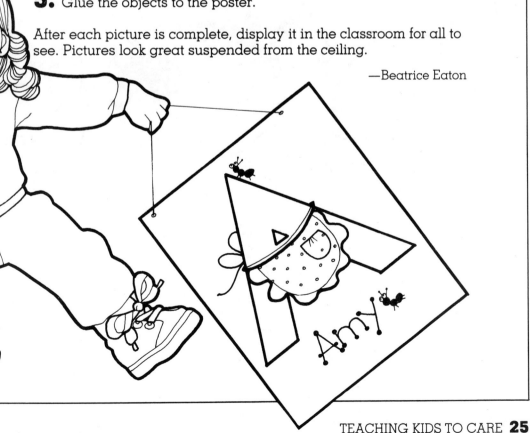

Pictionary of beginning sounds

BEHAVIORS: Cooperating, sharing (information and materials)

ACTIVITY: Beginning sounds

MATERIALS: magazines (with many pictures)   construction paper

scissors   glue   white paper

DIRECTIONS:

1. Prepare a blank book for the group to make a pictionary.

2. Provide the children with many magazines.

3. Tell the kids you will work together to find pictures that begin with the "B" sound.

4. Show pictures to the group to see if they can identify which have the "B" sounds.

5. Children find pictures and cut them out; they paste "B" pictures in the pictionary.

6. Continue the project until the pictionary is complete.

What if . . .

BEHAVIORS: Cooperating, sharing, rescuing, defending

ACTIVITY: Language and thinking game

MATERIALS: pictures

DIRECTIONS: **1.** Gather the children into a group and tell them you are going to play a game called "What If . . ."

2. Tell them you are going to show them pictures and they are to raise their hands and tell you what they think is happening in each picture, and tell you what they would do if it were happening in the school.

3. Show the children pictures you have cut out of:
a child crying
a child who has fallen
children playing while one child watches
a child being scolded for doing something wrong
a shy child

Our golden rules

BEHAVIORS: Cooperating, sharing information

ACTIVITY: Language experience activity

MATERIALS: chart paper

marker or crayon

DIRECTIONS: **1.** Write at the top of the paper: Our Golden Rules.

2. Begin a discussion about classroom rules. For example, what to do when walking into the room, how to act during play time, and so on.

3. Ask each child to contribute to the list of rules.

4. After the list is complete, ask each child to read his or her rule.

5. Post the rules in the classroom.

6. Review the rules daily for about one week.

Shape up

BEHAVIORS: Cooperating, sharing information

ACTIVITY: Word recognition (action words, number words), large motor

MATERIALS: action word flash cards   workout paper   pencils

DIRECTIONS: **1.** Begin by reviewing action words: jump, hop, skip, run, bend, gallop.

2. Divide children into pairs. Give each child a workout paper and a pencil.

3. One child "reads" the workout exercises as the other child completes each task. As they complete each task, it is checked off.

4. The youngsters then change places.

WORKOUT SHEET

_____ hop 3 times	_____ skip 6 times
_____ jump 4 times	_____ roll 8 times
_____ run 10 times	_____ gallop 4 times
	_____ slide 7 times

Great ideas

BEHAVIORS: Cooperating, sharing (information and materials), defending, rescuing

ACTIVITY: Oral language, brainstorming language experience

MATERIALS: pictures of situations demonstrating the different prosocial skills— firefighter rescuing a person, two kids sharing

DIRECTIONS: **1.** Each day during circle or transition time, show the group one of the pictures.

2. For each picture, ask the following questions:

● What do you think is happening?

● How do you think you could help?

CONTINUED

3. Write the children's responses on separate sheets of paper, and display under each picture on a bulletin board.

4. Review the pictures and kids' responses with individual children.

Preschool charades

BEHAVIOR: Cooperating

ACTIVITY: Word recognition game (action words)

MATERIALS: strips of construction paper   markers

DIRECTIONS:

1. Review action words.

2. Write and draw an action phrase on each strip of paper. Younger children can do this by having picture cards.

● hop like a (picture of bunny)

● throw a (picture of ball)

Some cards for older kids can have action words without pictures:

● run, crawl, sway, dance, jump

3. Each child receives an action strip and acts it out.

4. The other children try to guess what each child is doing.

5. If no one guesses, the child can give hints: "You eat this at lunch" (sandwich).

Hungry caterpillar

BEHAVIORS: Cooperating, sharing

ACTIVITY: Reading readiness, art, bulletin board

MATERIALS: oak tag   Velcro   felt   clear contact paper

large circles cut from white construction paper

DIRECTIONS:

1. Read *The Very Hungry Caterpillar* by Eric Carle (New York: Putnam Publishing Group, 1981) and discuss the life of a caterpillar, including what it eats.

2. Cut shapes of food eaten by the caterpillar from oak tag and cover with clear contact paper.

3. Arrange the food shapes on the table.

4. Now, after you have read the story, play a guessing game: Kids hide their eyes and you take away one of the food shapes, then ask a student to identify the missing food.

5. Youngsters each color in a circle shape. Place all of the circles together to make a hungry caterpillar for the bulletin board.

6. Children place the food shapes around the caterpillar.

—Deborah Cameron

Build a house

BEHAVIORS: Cooperating, sharing (information and materials)

ACTIVITY: Language development

MATERIALS: four pieces of white poster board

two pieces of brown poster board

home decorating magazines

glue

scissors

DIRECTIONS: **1.** At the bottom of each piece of white poster board write the name of a different room in a house (kitchen, bedroom, bathroom, living room).

2. Divide children into four groups and give each group a piece of poster board. Tell the kids in that group to look through the magazines and cut out pictures of objects that belong in the room on their poster board.

3. The children glue the room decorations on the poster board.

4. Staple the poster board pieces together to build a house.

5. Cut the brown poster board diagonally.

6. Staple the two pieces together to make a roof, and staple the roof to the house.

7. Hang the "house" on the wall.

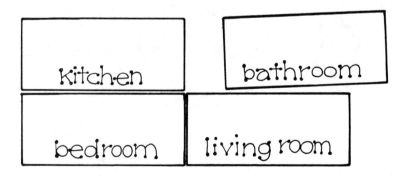

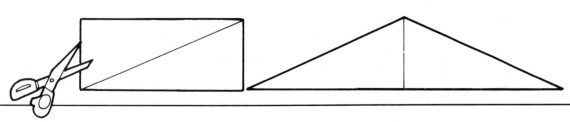

Prosocial stories
for
young children

What does cooperation mean? Do I share? How do you rescue or defend a friend? How can I comfort a child? What is a friend? Nothing teaches youngsters like a good book. The titles in this section have been selected because they help children explore the meaning of prosocial behaviors. There is a wealth of learning opportunities in each section. For your convenience, the books have been divided into six topics: sharing, comforting, cooperating, rescuing and defending, and friendship.

SHARING:

Claude the Dog by Dick Gackenbach. New York: Ticknor & Fields, 1982.

The Magic Porridge Pot by Paul Galdone. Boston: Houghton-Mifflin, 1976.

Mine, Yours, Ours by Burton Albert. Illus. by Lois Axeman. Chicago: Albert Whitman, 1977.

Rachel and Obadiah by Brinton Cassady Turkle. New York: Dutton, 1978.

The Smallest Boy in Class by Jerrold Beim. Illus. by Meg Wohlberg. New York: Morrow, 1949.

Tom Fox and the Apple Pie by Clyde Watson. Illus. by Wendy Watson. New York: Crowell Junior Books, 1979.

COOPERATION:

It's Mine by Leo Lionni. New York: Knopf, 1986.

Our Snowman by M. B. Goffstein. New York: Harper Junior Books, 1986.

COMFORT:

Go and Hush the Baby by Betsy Byars. New York: Viking, 1971.

I Had a Bad Dream by Linda Hayward. Illus. by Eugenie. New York: Western Publishing Co., 1985.

Jenny's in the Hospital by Seymour Reit. New York: Western Publishing Co., 1984.

Maybe a Band-Aid Will Help by Anna G. Hines. New York: Dutton, 1984.

Teddy Bears Cure a Cold by Susanna Gretz. Illus. by Alison Sage. New York: Macmillan, 1985.

RESCUE:

Fire! Fire! by Gail Gibbons. New York: Crowell Junior Books, 1984.

Don't Worry, I'll Find You by Anna Grossnickle Hines. New York: Dutton, 1986.

Island Rescue by Charles E. Martin. New York: Greenwillow, 1985.

FRIENDSHIP:

A Friend Is Someone Who Likes You by Joan Walsh Anglund. New York: Harcourt Brace Jovanovich, 1983.

Days with Frog and Toad by Arnold Lobel. New York: Harper Junior Books, 1985.

Do You Want to Be My Friend? by Eric Carle. New York: Crowell Junior Books, 1971.

Friends by Helme Heine. New York: Macmillan, 1986.

Frog and Toad All Year by Arnold Lobel. New York: Harper Junior Books, 1976.

KINDNESS:

The Foolish Giant by Bruce Coville and Katherine Coville. New York: Lippincott Junior Books, 1978.

Horton Hatches the Egg by Theodor Seuss Geisel. New York: Random House, 1940.

Horton Hears a Who by Theodor Seuss Geisel. New York: Random House, 1954.

The Country Bunny and the Little Gold Shoes by Du Bose Heyward. Boston: Houghton-Mifflin, 1939.

KINDNESS TO ANIMALS:

Amy's Goose by Efner Tudor Holmes. New York: Harper Junior Books, 1986.

The Little Lamb by Judy Dunn. New York: Random House, 1978.

Lonesome Little Colt by Clarence William Anderson. New York: Macmillan, 1974.

HELPFULNESS:

Elephant in a Well by Marie Hall Ets. New York: Viking, 1972.

The Tailor of Gloucester by Beatrix Potter. New York: Warne, 1968.

Timothy Turtle by Alice V. Davis. New York: Harcourt Brace Jovanovich, 1972.

What's the Matter with Carruthers? by James Marshall. Boston: Houghton-Mifflin, 1972.

Who's a Pest? by Crosby Newell Bonsall. New York: Harper Junior Books, 1962.

GENEROSITY:

Christmas Is a Time of Giving by Joan Walsh Anglund. New York: Harcourt Brace Jovanovich, 1961.

The Giving Tree by Shel Silverstein. New York: Harper Junior Books, 1964.

Little Bear's Christmas by Janice Brustlein. New York: Lothrop, Lee & Shepard Books, 1964.

The Mole Family's Christmas by Russell Conwell Hoban. New York: Scholastic, 1986.

Puppetry with a prosocial message

Puppetry and creative dramatics activities are ideal for the development of prosocial skills. They provide countless opportunities for sharing ideas and information, cooperating, helping, defending, rescuing, and comforting. So set the stage for prosocial development with the puppetry and creative dramatics ideas in this section. To reduce your preparation time, we've included easy-to-make puppet patterns and suggestions for collecting or making props.

Meet the prosocial puppets

Role-playing with puppets is an ideal way to help children act out prosocial behaviors. Use the puppet patterns on the pages following; let the children give a fun name to each puppet as it relates to a specific prosocial behavior. Laminate or cover each pattern with clear contact paper, then glue a cardboard strip or wooden dowel to the back to create a stick puppet.

Here are some ways you can use your puppets with your youngsters:

● **Introduce each puppet separately.** Over a period of a week or two, welcome each puppet as a new member of the class. Make the introductions with enthusiasm, so the children are eager to model the prosocial behavior.

● **Make the prosocial puppets come alive.** Use your voice to develop a unique personality for each character. Then have the character speak to the kids about his or her behavior toward others.

● **Role-play real-life situations with the characters.** Explain to the children that they are going to get a chance to hold the puppet and talk to him or her during a short role-playing situation.

Using the puppet who acts as the comforter as an example, have one child hold and talk for the puppet. Ask another child to pretend to cry after falling in the gym. This puppet approaches the child and says in his or her soft, soothing voice, ''What's wrong? Why are you crying?'' The injured youngster answers that he or she has fallen and has hurt himself or herself. Your puppet comforts the child and assures him or her that the hurt will go away soon and that everything will be fine again.

● **Set up a prosocial puppet area.** After introducing the puppets, place them in a special center. Provide times when children can play with the puppets. Put up a puppet stage and have as many props as possible out for the children to choose from.

● **Be prepared when prosocial classroom problems arise.** Many classroom situations will occur that involve cooperating, helping, sharing, defending, rescuing, and comforting. After the situation is resolved, use the appropriate prosocial puppet or puppets to talk to the children. Each puppet can use its unique personality to help the kids understand the situation.

Friends at play

BEHAVIORS: Rescuing, comforting, helping

ACTIVITY: Puppetry

MATERIALS: poem (attached)

construction paper for scenery

girl and boy puppet shapes cut from our patterns

dowel rods   tape   crayons   sheet

DIRECTIONS:

1. Read the following poem to children several times.

2. Children make scenery for puppetry activity by using construction paper to make trees, a sun, a house, birds, and hills. It is helpful to give younger children a pattern to trace.

3. The youngsters arrange their pieces on a sheet to make a background.

4. Next they make their own puppets by coloring in a puppet shape.

5. Tape dowel rods to paper puppets.

6. Read the poem and ask two children to act out the story. Try to get the children to say what their puppet says in the poem.

7. As a follow-up activity, ask the kids if they ever felt lonely and needed a friend to play with. If so, what did they do?

"FRIENDS AT PLAY": POEM

One beautiful and sunny day
A little girl sat under a tree waiting for a
   friend to play.

She watched as the clouds floated by
And pretended she could fly so very high.

She flew above the trees and housetops
And around the sun with one big flip flop.

But as much as she liked flying like birds
All she wanted were a few friendly
   words.

Just when she was ready to cry
A little boy came running by.

He stopped and asked, "Would you like to
   play?"
She smiled and said, "I've been waiting
   all day!"

So together they ran and played in the
   grass
But oh so quickly the time did pass.

And soon it was time to call it a day
But tomorrow there will be more time to
   play!

—Deborah Cameron

Reproducible pattern for puppets

DIRECTIONS:
Use oak tag or poster board for puppet shapes. Children can draw the face or glue on construction paper shapes for eyes, nose, and mouth. Pieces of yarn may be used for hair.

Puppet clothing patterns

DIRECTIONS:
Use fabric scraps to cut out dresses and overalls for puppets. Let children decorate clothes with small buttons, ric rac, ribbon, and sequins. This can be applied to fabric with craft glue.

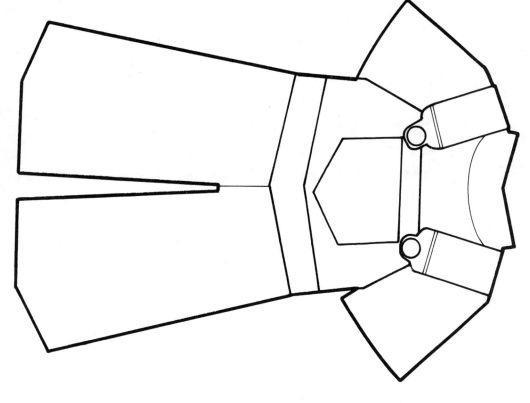

Firefighter puppets

BEHAVIORS: Rescuing, cooperating

ACTIVITY: Puppetry/creative dramatics

MATERIALS:
paper bags   scraps of paper (for clothing and
glue   facial features)
crayons   large box

DIRECTIONS:

1. Cut out holes in a box to make windows for a building.

2. Cut out paper flames which children glue in the window.

3. Cut out firefighters with uniforms and facial features, and other people.

4. Children paste a helmet to the top of a paper bag, a uniform to the center, and facial features to the bottom (what the bag would sit on) to make firefighters.

5. Then the kids paste facial features to the bottoms of bags for people to be rescued.

6. Divide children into two groups: firefighters and people to be rescued.

7. Children act out the rescue of people from a burning building by the firefighters.

8. Firefighters respond to the call of "Help" and rescue the people from the burning building.

9. People in the building cry for help and try to remain calm while escaping safely.

10. Have children switch roles so that all have a chance to act in both roles.

—Beatrice Eaton

Patterns for firefighter puppets

Mr. Happy/Mr. Sad

BEHAVIORS: Sharing, comforting

ACTIVITY: Puppetry

MATERIALS: blue and yellow construction paper cut into 2½" circles

Popsicle sticks

glue or tape

markers or crayons

DIRECTIONS:

1. Give each child a yellow and blue circle and a Popsicle stick.

2. Kids draw a happy face on the yellow circle and a sad face on the blue circle.

3. Tape the Popsicle stick on the back of one circle, then the children may glue the back of the other one to the stick, too.

4. Kids bring their puppets to the circle and listen to short stories which describe different situations. They use their puppets to express how they feel about the situation. Examples are on the next page.

5. Youngsters may keep the puppets in their special compartments and use them when they need comforting or want to share good or bad news.

—Deborah Cameron

Situations to be used with Happy/Sad Puppets:

● **One rainy day Sally was very lonely** and couldn't find anything to do. Sally's mother asked her if she would like to have a friend over. Sally said yes, so her mother called Sally's friend Lisa. Lisa wasn't home so Sally's mother said they would have to do it another day.

● **Paul was very excited.** It was a special day: his birthday. He had waited a long time for this day to come, and now he was getting dressed because it was almost time for his fifth birthday party.

● **John was playing with his dump truck.** He loved to use it in his sand box. He made roads and mountains and pretended he was in a far-away country.

● **Susie loved to read stories about kittens.** She also collected kittens of all sizes and colors. Today when Susie's daddy came home he had a special surprise for Susie: her very own kitten named Mittens.

● **Laura was building a tall tower** with her new building blocks. She put windows in it and a flag at the top. Billy, Laura's brother, ran into the room and tripped over her tower, sending the blocks flying to the ground. Laura's tower was ruined.

Helping hand puppets

BEHAVIORS: Cooperating, helping (defending, sharing, rescuing)

ACTIVITY: Puppetry, creative dramatics

MATERIALS:

old socks	yarn	scissors
felt	rubber bands	glue
material scraps	face patterns	newspaper

DIRECTIONS:

1. Stuff the foot of an old sock with newspaper to make a puppet's head. Close the foot with a rubber band.

2. Cut holes on both sides of the sock, below the head, to use for finger holes.

3. Make faces with pieces of felt.

4. Children choose felt pieces and glue them to their sock puppet to make a face.

5. Give children yarn and material scraps to make hair and clothes for their puppets.

6. Discuss with the group a situation in which children would have to think about what they would do. For example, "What would you do if your friend spilled his milk?"

7. Give each child a chance to respond with his or her puppet.

—Margaret Bermens

Five woolly caterpillars

BEHAVIOR: Cooperating

ACTIVITY: Science finger play

MATERIALS:
finger play
paper plates (9")
eyes and antennas cut from construction paper
cotton balls dyed brown (place in bag with dry brown tempera)
dowel rods   watered-down glue
tape   paint brushes

DIRECTIONS:
1. Choose five children, and let each child say one part of the finger play and do the actions.

2. The whole group says the last two lines together.

3. Give each child a paper plate, and ask him or her to glue two antennas and two eyes on the plate.

4. Use a paint brush to cover the paper plate with watered-down glue.

5. Apply brown cotton balls to the plate, pulling the balls apart to make them fluffy.

—Deborah Cameron

"FIVE WOOLLY CATERPILLARS"

Five woolly caterpillars went out crawling (wiggle 5 fingers).
The first one said, "The leaves are falling" (flutter fingers and move hands
   downward).
The second one said, "I feel a chill in the air" (wrap arms around body).
The third one said, "But what do we care?" (shrug shoulders).
The fourth one said, "Soon winter will be here" (rub hands together).
The fifth one said, "See you next year" (wave good-bye).

Five woolly caterpillars all crawled away;
Maybe we'll see them again some warm spring day.

Crossing the street

BEHAVIORS: Cooperating, rescuing (safety)

ACTIVITY: Creative dramatics

MATERIALS: none

DIRECTIONS: **1.** Do the finger play for the children slowly, demonstrating the motions. Ask children to join in the second time around.

When we cross the street,
We look both ways (look to one side and then to other).
We always walk, we never run (walk fingers).
We take our time; we'll get there okay.
If we see a car (point to eyes)
We better stay (hold up hand).

—Beatrice Eaton

Dial 911

BEHAVIOR: Rescuing

ACTIVITY: Creative dramatics (teaching children to dial an emergency number and to talk to police)

MATERIALS:

police hat	dress-up clothes
desk	medical kit
three telephones	

DIRECTIONS:

1. After a lesson in which kids learn how to say their addresses and phone numbers, discuss with them how to call the police in an emergency. On a play telephone, give each youngster a chance to practice dialing 911.

2. Pretend that a section of the classroom is a house with the child and his or her mother in it.

3. Across the room have a desk with a telephone on it and another child as a police officer sitting at the desk.

4. In another section have an ambulance driver and a telephone.

5. Describe this situation to the children:
A mother and child are at home. The mother falls and hurts herself badly. The child must go to the phone and dial 911. The police department answers. The child tells the officer, "My mother is hurt. I need help. Please come to (address and phone number)." The police officer calls the ambulance driver who brings two paramedics to the house.

6. Have the children act out the situation.

Away we go

BEHAVIOR: Cooperating, sharing (information and materials), rescuing

ACTIVITY: Creative dramatics, activity on transportation

MATERIALS: several cardboard boxes

chairs

hats— sailor

bus driver

airplane pilot

taxi driver

pictures of various means of transportation

DIRECTIONS: **1.** Discuss the various means of transportation by using the pictures.

2. Put the boxes, hats, and chairs in the middle of the room.

3. Divide the children into several groups: Give each group a box and hats for each mode of transportation.

4. Tell each group of children that they are to work together with the boxes, chairs, and hats to take a "trip."

Have a campout

BEHAVIORS: Cooperating, sharing (information and materials)

ACTIVITY: Creative dramatics

MATERIALS: several large boxes   backpacks

blankets   outdoor cooking utensils

sheets   long pieces of rope

firewood

DIRECTIONS: **1.** Before campout day discuss camping out, show pictures, and make a list of items that campers need.

2. Depending on the size of the group, divide children into buddy groups of three or four.

3. Each group has a "tent" (a large box), blankets, sheets (for the front of the tent), and other camping equipment.

4. The group members work together to set up a camp site.

5. The whole group builds a "fire" from the firewood, "cooks" dinner, and sings songs around the camp fire.

Working together for math readiness

Math readiness activities, so important to your early childhood curriculum, naturally encourage children to work together in problem-solving situations. In this section, children team up to count and identify numerals. These activities will help you see if your youngsters understand basic math concepts while they share, cooperate, and help each other. Sharpen math and prosocial skills with these preschool-tested activities.

A C T I V I T Y

Hunt for snacks

BEHAVIOR: Cooperating

ACTIVITY: Counting

MATERIALS: plates of snacks—small bags of raisins, pretzels, peanuts

containers of juice   cups   napkins

DIRECTIONS:
1. Have two children count out enough cups and napkins for the group and fill the snack plates with raisins, pretzels, and peanuts.

2. Hide the snacks, cups, napkins, and juice around the room when the children are not there.

3. Tell the group to find everything and place the items on the table.

4. Place a bowl on the table to pour all of the snacks into.

5. The group then sits down and passes around the cups, napkins, snacks, and juice. Wait until everyone is served before eating.

Contain it

BEHAVIOR: Cooperating

ACTIVITY: Sorting, organizing, and word recognition

MATERIALS: adhesive labels

square tissue boxes with tops removed

marker

DIRECTIONS: **1.** Label the tissue boxes with what they are to hold: red markers, yellow crayons, scissors, blue crayons, and so on.

2. Provide the opportunity for the group to work together to sort and organize the classroom materials into each box.

Take a poll

BEHAVIOR: Cooperating

ACTIVITY: Math readiness

MATERIALS: large poster board

DIRECTIONS: **1.** Introduce a question to the class. It should involve something familiar to them. Make questionnaires written in picture form.

2. Poll the children in the class. This can be done by hand vote or by having the children fill out the questionnaire.

3. Give kids questionnaires to take home for their family members.

4. Tally and record results on poster board.

5. Send home results of the poll when the question has been answered.

—Deborah Cameron

Save the sailors

BEHAVIORS: Cooperating, rescuing

ACTIVITY: Math readiness bulletin board

MATERIALS: 10 boats

10 sails

55 sailors

DIRECTIONS: **1.** Cut out sailors, sails, and boats:

Number the boats from 1 to 10.

Number the sails from 1 to 10.

Place the sailboats on the bulletin board.

Place sailors in an envelope and staple it to the bulletin board.

Place sails in an envelope and staple it to the opposite corner of the bulletin board.

2. Children pick out a sail and match the number on the sail to the sailboat.

3. Kids then count out all of the sailors until all are rescued and put them in the boat. The number of sailors matches the numbers on the boat.

—Beatrice Eaton

Save the sailors

REPRODUCIBLE SAILOR PATTERN

Save the sailors

REPRODUCIBLE SAILBOAT
PATTERN

1

Scavenger hunt

BEHAVIORS: Cooperating, helping

ACTIVITY: Math readiness

MATERIALS: two sheets of paper with a picture list of items to collect

include such items as blocks, dominoes, pieces of chalk

DIRECTIONS: **1.** Place items around the room.

2. Divide the class into two or three teams. Try to make teams with four or five students on them.

3. Pass out the list of things to find. Go over the list making sure that each team knows what the pictures are.

4. Explain that each member of the team needs to help retrieve the items.

5. Show children where collected items should be placed for each team.

6. You must help younger children while they are collecting their items so each team member gets a turn. Team members enjoy helping each other find the items.

7. When all teams have collected their items, check the scavenger list to make sure that everything was collected.

— Deborah Cameron

Matching prints

BEHAVIORS: Cooperating, helping

ACTIVITY: Matching and left/right game

MATERIALS: construction paper—a different color for each child

marker

scissors

DIRECTIONS:

1. Two children should work together. One child traces the other child's hands to make handprints. Then they switch places.

2. Each child cuts out his or her own prints.

3. Each youngster holds on to the left handprint. Right handprints for the entire group are placed in a bag. You shake the bag.

4. Children take turns drawing out a right handprint, then matching it with the child holding the left handprint. It is best to have one child go around at a time matching the prints.

Gum fun for the school

BEHAVIORS: Cooperating, sharing

ACTIVITY: Counting

MATERIALS: colored construction paper

white poster board

glue

scissors

DIRECTIONS:

1. Make a large gum machine from the pattern on the next page.

2. Cut small round bubblegum shapes from different colors of construction paper.

3. Children count the pieces of "gum."

4. Kids then glue the "gum" on the poster board machine.

5. On a Monday, hang the gum machine in a central location so that all of the children in the school can guess how many pieces of "gum" are in the machine.

6. By Wednesday, each class in the school should have estimated one number for the pieces of "gum."

7. On Friday, write the correct number above the machine along with the winning class.

8. The winners win the machine.

Gumball machine

Our frosty

BEHAVIORS: Sharing, cooperating

ACTIVITY: Math (big, bigger, biggest)

MATERIALS:

warm clothes for children	3 cardboard circles (big, bigger, biggest)
hat	raisins
neck scarf	two small stones
fresh snow	three large stones
carrot	two long sticks

DIRECTIONS:

1. Everyone put on warm clothes and boots to go outside on a snowy day.

2. Divide children into three groups when you are outside.

3. Place one of the three circles in front of each group.

4. Explain to the children that they are to work together to make a round ball of snow as large as their cardboard circle.

5. Stack the snowballs on top of each other—first biggest, next bigger, then big.

6. The children can decorate the snowman with small stones for eyes and mouth, a carrot for a nose, a real hat and scarf.

7. Bring the kids inside; gather them together and decide on a name for their new friend.

Add a flower

BEHAVIORS: Cooperating, sharing (information and materials)

ACTIVITY: Math readiness—numbers; spring

MATERIALS:

20 3-inch paper circles	glue
colored construction paper	scissors
flower petal patterns	marker

DIRECTIONS:

1. Write the numbers 1-10 on the paper circles, making two of each number.

2. Review the numbers 1-10 with the class by showing the class each circle and matching the correct number of paper petals to it. Glue the petals on to make May flowers.

3. Hang the flowers where the children can easily see them.

4. Divide the class into five groups. Give each group two of the numbered circles and plenty of paper petals.

5. Have groups make flowers with the correct number of petals to match their circles, by gluing petals to the circle.

6. Display the flowers on a spring bulletin board.

—Margaret Bermens

PATTERN

May flowers patterns

NUMBER CIRCLE

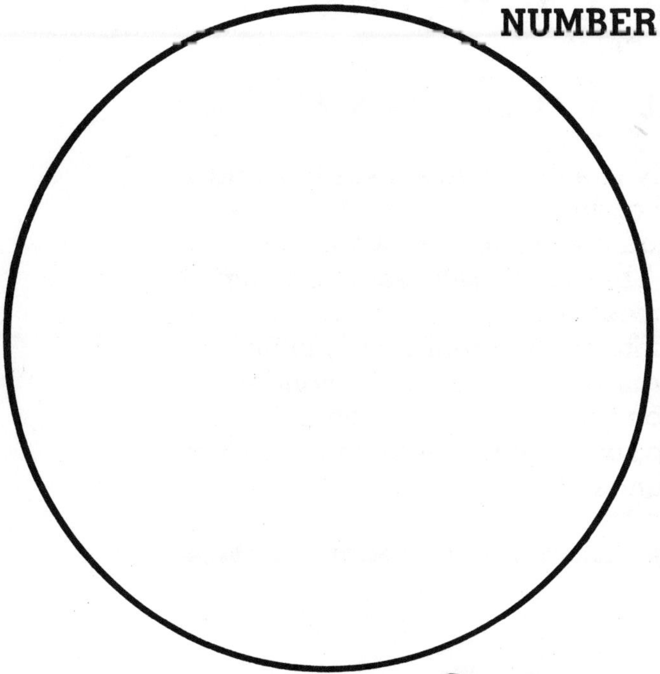

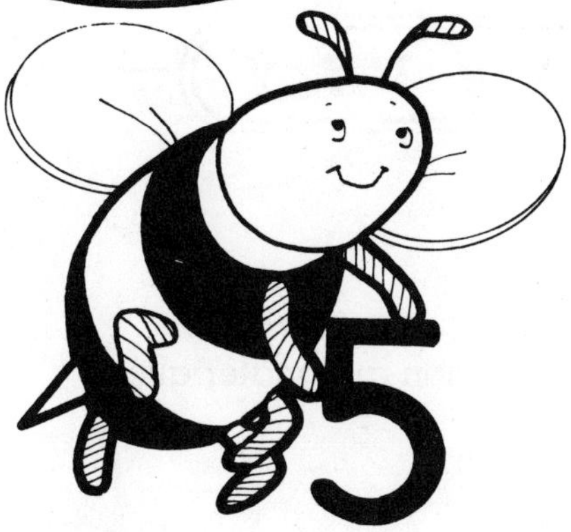

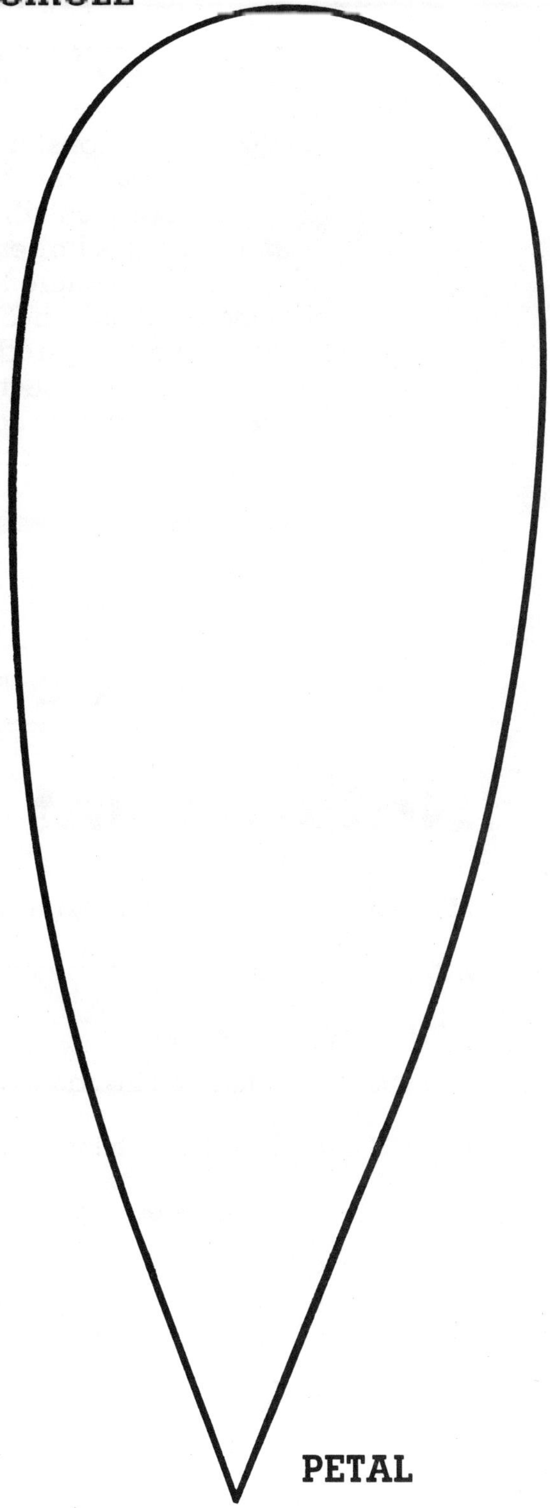

PETAL

Working together to discover our world

Children constantly use their five senses to explore and discover the environment. When they enter an early childhood program, their world becomes larger. There is more to see, hear, smell, taste, and feel. Nature takes on a new meaning. And what makes these encounters with nature even more exciting? Exploring and discovering scientific wonders with friends. In this section you'll find hands-on activities designed to reinforce cooperating and helping behaviors while teaching basic science skills.

ACTIVITY

Nature hunt

BEHAVIORS: Cooperating, sharing (information and materials)

ACTIVITY: Science/discovery—nature hunt

MATERIALS: paper bags

nature picture cards (word cards may also be used)

DIRECTIONS: **1.** Divide children into groups of three.

2. Give each group several picture cards of objects found in nature, such as leaves, acorns, and pine cones.

3. The groups find the objects on their picture cards and place them in the bags.

4. In the classroom each group glues its objects on a nature chart with the picture or word card below it.

—Margaret Bermens

Dress Bruno, the Weather Bear

BEHAVIORS: Cooperating, helping, sharing (information)

ACTIVITY: Science/discovery (circle time)

MATERIALS: large bear pattern glued to a background

clothes for the season (see patterns)

DIRECTIONS: **1.** Take the children outside for a few moments so they can see and feel what type of day it is. If it's very cold outside, you might just want to look out the window.

2. Have a group discussion about what clothing Bruno, the Weather Bear, would wear if he went outside.

3. Give each child a ditto sheet of Bruno. Kids cut out the clothes and glue them on Bruno and pretend that he is going outside.

—Beatrice Eaton

Bruno the Weather Bear

PATTERN OF BRUNO

Bruno the Weather Bear

PATTERN FOR BRUNO'S RAIN GEAR

Bruno the Weather Bear

PATTERN FOR BRUNO'S WINTER CLOTHES

Bruno the Weather Bear

PATTERN FOR BRUNO'S SUMMER CLOTHES

Them bones

BEHAVIORS: Cooperating, helping

ACTIVITY: Science/discovery—a unit on the human body which requires children to create a skeleton

MATERIALS: song: "Them Bones"

bones of oaktag: skull, shoulder, arms, hands, ribs, hips, legs, feet (see patterns)

brads

ditto sheet with skeleton outlined, with numbered parts

paper bones numbered to match the ditto

glue

DIRECTIONS: **1.** Give each child a large paper bone.

2. Have children attach their bones with the brads as they are mentioned in the song. For example, "The hand bone's connected to the arm bone"—the child with the hand bone attaches it to the arm bone already in place.

3. The skeleton is hung in the room as a decoration.

4. As a follow-up activity the children move to the table so they can make their own skeletons by matching the numbers on the bones to the numbers on their ditto diagram.

5. Sing the song again as a group.

SONG: "THEM BONES"

1. Start by having one child tape the skull to the wall or bulletin board.

2. Give each child one large bone.

3. Everybody sings the following song and demonstrates the words.

The skull bone's connected to the neck bone.
(child attaches neck and shoulder bone to skull)
The shoulder bone's connected to the arm bone.
(child attaches arm to shoulder bone)
The arm bone's connected to the hand bone.
The shoulder bone's connected to the rib cage.
The rib cage's connected to the hip bone.
The hip bone's connected to the leg bone.
The leg bone's connected to the foot bone.

—Deborah Cameron

Them bones

PATTERN OF SKELETON

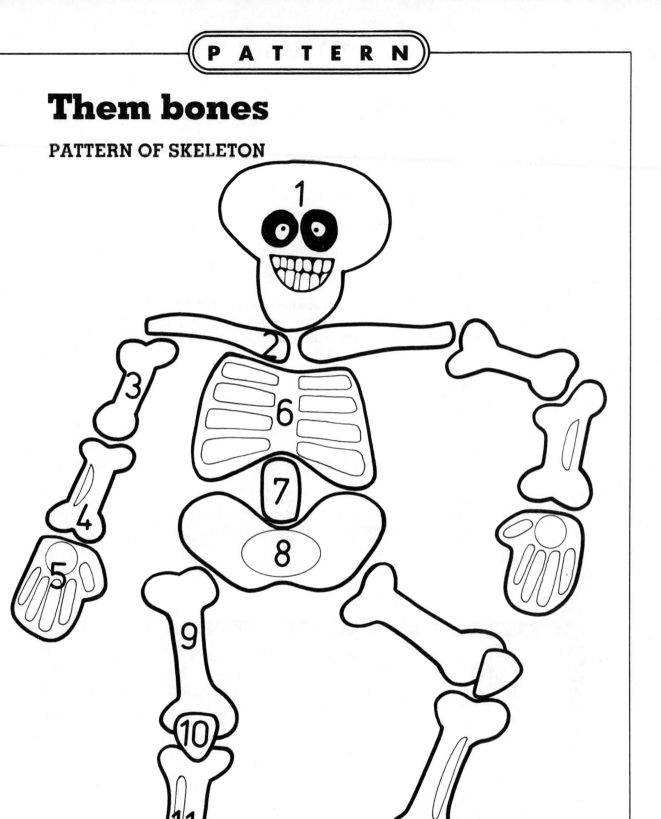

Create a classroom aquarium

BEHAVIORS: Cooperating, sharing (information and materials)

ACTIVITY: Science bulletin board

MATERIALS: patterns for aquarium creatures   markers
different colors of construction paper   glue
two pieces of light blue construction paper   scissors

DIRECTIONS:

1. Children use the various patterns on the following pages to trace and cut out the animal and plant life for an aquarium. One group should be responsible for the animals and one for the plants.

2. Staple the two pieces of light blue poster board together.

3. Cut out ½-inch strips of black construction paper to staple around the posterboard to resemble an aquarium.

4. Children in each group place their animals and plants in the aquarium.

5. Also suggest they get a real aquarium, if possible, and have kids share responsibilities in keeping it clean and feeding the fish.

Aquarium creatures

PATTERNS FOR ANIMALS IN AN AQUARIUM

Aquarium creatures

PATTERNS FOR MORE AQUARIUM CREATURES

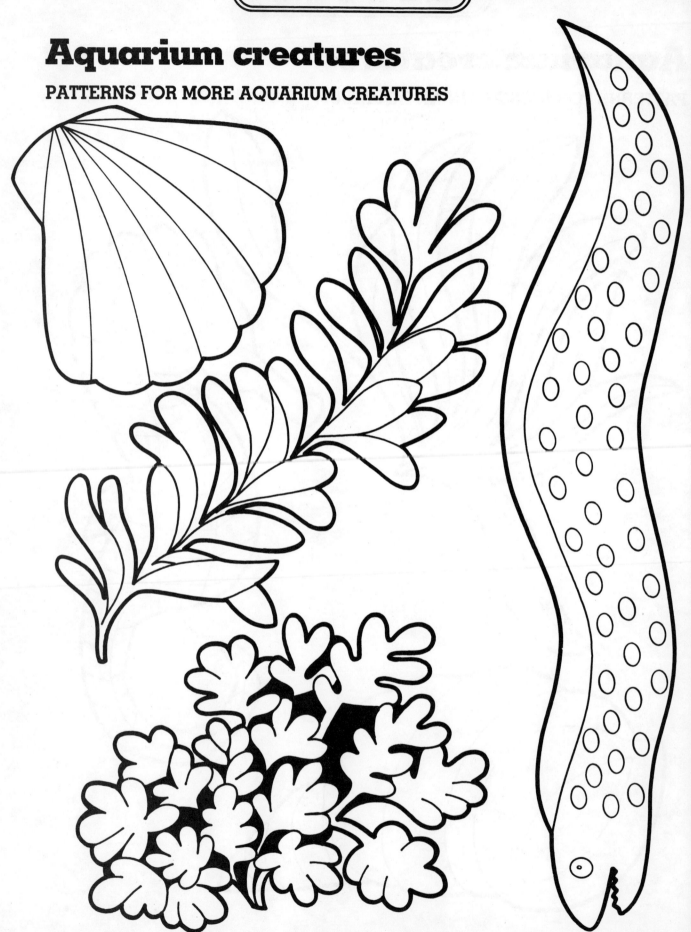

Aquarium creatures

PATTERNS FOR MORE AQUARIUM CREATURES

Colors, colors everywhere

BEHAVIORS: Cooperating, sharing (information and materials)

ACTIVITY: Science

MATERIALS: red, blue, and yellow paint · poster board · paper · paint cups · brushes · markers · droppers

DIRECTIONS:

1. Make a chart showing the mixing of primary colors and the result. For example, Red + Yellow = Orange. Beneath the name of the color, paint a dot with that color.

2. Give several small groups of children cups of red, blue, and yellow paint with a dropper in each cup. Make sure they have empty cups, too.

3. Let the youngsters make new colors by following the directions on the chart.

4. Each group then makes one color mural with all of the newly mixed colors.

—Margaret Bermens

How does your garden grow?

BEHAVIORS: Comforting, sharing (information and materials)

ACTIVITY: Science

MATERIALS: box · soil · water bottle · seeds (marigolds or other fast-growing seeds) · Styrofoam cups

DIRECTIONS:

1. Children each fill their cups with soil and plant several seeds, water the soil, and place the cups in the sunlight.

2. The children must check the soil each day to make sure it is moist.

3. When the plant grows and flowers begin to bloom, each child gives his or her flower to a special friend or family member for a special gift.

—Beatrice Eaton

Plant puzzle

BEHAVIORS: Cooperating, sharing

ACTIVITY: Science—discovering plants

MATERIALS: large laminated puzzle of plant with parts labeled: root, stem, leaves, flower

tape   glue   scissors

crayons   small plastic kitchen bags

DIRECTIONS: **1.** Draw, color, and label a large picture of a plant (see flower garden patterns) on poster board. Cover with clear contact paper and cut into five or six pieces.

2. Tape the puzzle to chalkboard so the children can see the whole picture. Name four different parts: root, stem, leaves, and flower.

3. Give each student a piece of the puzzle.

4. One at a time the children put their pieces on the board, naming that part. You may have to put the puzzle together more than once so everyone gets a turn.

5. When the large puzzle is completed, review the four parts of the plant. Leave the whole puzzle on the board for a model.

6. Children move to the table to color their own plant pictures.

7. Kids are given the four labels to place on the appropriate parts of their puzzles.

8. Cut each picture into five or six pieces of a puzzle, and put the pieces in plastic bags.

9. Youngsters exchange bags and build the new puzzles.

—Deborah Cameron

Leaf person

BEHAVIORS: Cooperating, sharing (information and materials)

ACTIVITY: Science

MATERIALS: leaves   markers

brown wrapping paper   glue

DIRECTIONS: **1.** On a large piece of brown wrapping paper, draw a person, complete with arms, legs, hands, feet, and facial features. Set this aside.

2. Go on a neighborhood walk with the children and collect leaves of different colors.

3. When everyone returns, the kids should sort the leaves according to their colors.

4. Show the children the person drawn on the large sheet of wrapping paper.

5. Discuss the different parts of the body and have children point to their own body parts.

6. The kids decide what color of leaves they would like to paste on the different body parts—for example, yellow for hair, brown for pants.

7. Have children paste the leaves to the body.

8. When their leaf friend is dry, hang him or her in the hallway or classroom for everyone to enjoy.

Grow a winter flower garden

BEHAVIORS: Cooperating, sharing (materials and information)

ACTIVITY: Science

MATERIALS: piece of Styrofoam 48" x 24"

colored construction paper

flower patterns on the following pages

green pipe cleaners

dark brown paint

DIRECTIONS:

1. Divide children into groups of three.

2. Set up activity centers around the room for groups to:

a. Paint the Styrofoam brown like the ground.

b. Cut and trace paper flowers from the patterns.

3. Attach the pipe cleaner stems to the flowers and "plant" them in the styrofoam. Kids will enjoy seeing their colorful make-believe garden in the middle of winter.

Let's share a song

Songs and finger plays add life to any early childhood learning experience. They make youngsters laugh, dance, clap, sing, hum, and move. This happy atmosphere becomes a perfect springboard for teaching a variety of concepts. The songs, finger plays, and poems in this section were created to teach and reinforce prosocial skills. You'll discover old familiar tunes with new words about friendship, helping, rescuing, defending, and cooperating. Each of the songs is accompanied by a fun-to-do activity.

New friends

BEHAVIOR: Friendship

ACTIVITY: Developing large motor skills

MATERIALS: none

DIRECTIONS:

1. Teach the song to the children. Tell them they are going to learn a special dance to greet a new friend, then sing the song with them.

2. Have everyone form a circle and circle left while a new student stands in the center. Sing the song, circling to the left during the first verse of the song.

3. During the second verse, everyone circles to the right until the end of the song.

Now sing this song to the tune of "Twinkle, Twinkle, Little Star."

VERSE 1:
Come little children make a circle
All around our new friend Sammy.
She's as nice as she can be—
Raise our hands and clap to three.
(Kids raise hands and clap three times overhead.)
Come little children make a circle
All around our new friend Sammy.

VERSE 2:
Come, little Sammy, can't you see
We enjoy your company.
Join our circle, one, two, three—
(The new child joins the circle.)
We'll be friends, just wait and see.
Come little Sammy, can't you see
We enjoy your company.

—Debra Barger

We are all special F-R-I-E-N-D-S

BEHAVIOR: Friendship

ACTIVITY: Spelling, discussing friends

MATERIALS: pictures of kids playing

DIRECTIONS: Show pictures of children playing together and talk about how important friends are to each other. Does each child have a special friend? Are we all friends at our school? Discuss what kids can do with their special friends.

Make cards with one letter on each card to spell "FRIENDS." Distribute them to seven kids and have them try to arrange the letters in the correct spelling order. Repeat until all children have had a chance. When they all succeed, the whole class can learn this song.

Sing this song to the tune of "She'll Be Coming 'Round the Mountain."

VERSE 1:   We are all special fri-ends, yes we are.
We are all special fri-ends, yes we are.
We are different sizes and shapes;
We are different colors and makes—
But, we are all special fri-ends, yes we are.

VERSE 2:   We will all play together, yes we will.
We will all play together, yes we will.
Some can sing and some can run;
But we all can have great fun
We will all play together, yes we will.

VERSE 3:   Oh, we're happy to be together, yes we are.
Oh, we're happy to be together, yes we are.
We don't have to be the same;
We can laugh and play some games.
Oh, we're happy to be together, yes we are.

—Debra Barger

Helping

BEHAVIOR: Helping

ACTIVITY: Discussing how to help

MATERIALS: magazine pictures of people helping other people

DIRECTIONS: Show pictures of children helping people such as mothers, fathers, teachers, doctors. Talk about how important helping other people can be. How do they help their mothers? Who else can they help?

Next, talk about the many different reasons why they help someone. Then sing the song.

Sing this song to the music of "Frère Jacques."

Words by Debra Barger

1. I can help my teacher, I can help my teacher, Pick up the toys, Pick up the toys. She will be so proud of me, She will be so proud of me. When they're put away, When they're put away.

2. I can help my mother, I can help my mother, Clean up my room, Clean up my room. She will be so proud of me, She will be so proud of me. When it is done, When it is done.

3. I can help my father, I can help my father, Do the wash, Do the wash. He will be so proud of me, He will be so proud of me. When I help, When I help.

My little friend

To the tune of "Little Green Frog"

BEHAVIOR: Comforting

ACTIVITY: Discussing the concept of comforting and then discussing how to comfort friends

MATERIALS: none

DIRECTIONS: Sing the song with the children. Explain that friends can comfort other friends by just holding each other's hand. What are other ways to comfort a friend? Who else can the kids comfort?

VERSE 1. "When I see little friend sitting on the wall" (Have one student sit off by him- or herself. In the next phrase, have one friend walk over to the friend sitting by him- or herself.)

VERSE 2. First phrase, have both children sit together. Second phrase, have the children laugh. Third phrase, have the two friends stand. Fourth phrase, circle around together.

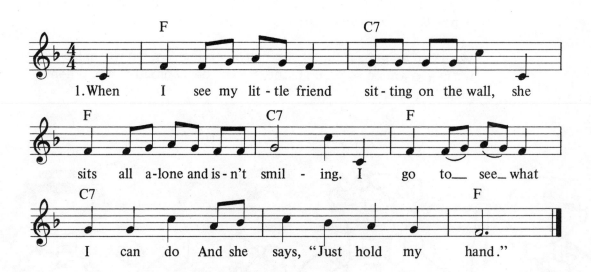

1. When I see my lit-tle friend sit-ting on the wall, she
sits all a-lone and is-n't smil-ing. I go to__ see__ what
I can do And she says, "Just hold my hand."

2. Now my friend and I are sitting on the wall.
   We sit together and laugh.
   I'm glad I found out what I could do,
   All she said was, "Hold my hand."

Give a smile

BEHAVIOR: Giving

ACTIVITY: Discussing how to give

MATERIALS: paper, crayons, or markers

DIRECTIONS: Sing the song with the children. Teach one verse at a time. Ask the children what the word "giving" means. Explain what you think "giving" really means. Ask the children what they could give to someone.

Have the children color a picture for someone they know. When they are finished, write the name of their friend on the picture and let the children take the picture to give to that person.

Here are the words of the song sung to the tune of "Eentsy, Weentsy Spider":

1. Give a little help to your next door neighbor. Give a little smile to your best friend. They will ~~return these wonderful favors, by saying,~~ do the same for you "Thanks again."

2. Give a little hug to someone who is crying. Give a little time to someone who is lonely. They will return these wonderful favors, by saying, "Thanks again."

Words by Debra Barger

If you see a friend in trouble

BEHAVIOR: Rescuing

ACTIVITY: Role-playing

MATERIALS: none

DIRECTIONS: Sing the following song with the children. Discuss with them how they can help a friend—or even a stranger— in trouble.

Have the kids act out how they would rescue someone. For example, have one child sit in a chair. That child rocks back a little bit too far in the chair. Another child stops the child from falling. See if the children can think of ways they can help keep their friends out of danger.

Here are the words to the song sung to the tune of "Go in and out the Window."

Words by Debra Barger

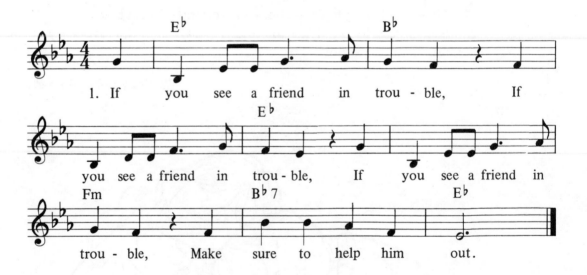

1. If you see a friend in trou - ble,
   If you see a friend in trou - ble,
   If you see a friend in trou - ble,
   Make sure to help him out.

2. We don't want to see a friend hurt,
   We don't want to see a friend hurt,
   We don't want to see a friend hurt,
   Make sure to help her out.

It is time

BEHAVIOR: Cooperation

ACTIVITY: Learning how to clean up

MATERIALS: none

DIRECTIONS: Sing the song with the children. Discuss what should happen at the end of the day. Show and tell the kids the correct way of putting things away.

Explain that at the end of the day their parents or friends will pick them up. Also remind them that they will be able to come back another day to play.

Here are the words to the song sung to the tune of "If You're Happy."

1. It is time for us to put our toys away (Away). It is time for us to put our toys away (Away). It is time for us to say, That we'll play another day, It is time for us to put our toys away (Away).

2. It is time for us to say good-bye (Good-bye). It is time for us to say good-bye (Good-bye). It is time for us to say, That we'll play another day, It is time for us to say good-bye (Good-bye).

Words by Debra Barger

What can we do

BEHAVIOR: Sharing

ACTIVITY: Learning to play different things together

MATERIALS: none

DIRECTIONS: Sing the song with the children. Have the youngsters form a circle. During the chorus, have them move to the left. During the verses, have the children act out what is being sung while maintaining the circle formation.

You may want to discuss what other things you can do at your school. Then add other verses accordingly.

Here are the words to the song sung to the tune of "The Mulberry Bush."

What can we do here at our school, here at our school, here at our school, What can we do here at our school with our special friend.

1. This is the way we march like a soldier, march like a soldier, march like a soldier, This is the way we march like a soldier with our special friend.

2. This is the way we dance like a doll.

3. This is the way we zoom like a car.

4. This is the way we build with blocks.

Words by Debra Barger

A C T I V I T Y

Together

BEHAVIOR: Cooperation

ACTIVITY: Discussing how to share and work together

MATERIALS: white sheet, food coloring, water, empty mustard bottle

DIRECTIONS: Sing the song with the children. Talk to them about how to work and share together. Ask them what kinds of things can be shared? How can everybody work together?

Spread the white sheet out on the floor. Children should share the bottle or bottles, depending on how many students are working together on this project. Let the children squirt the mixture on the sheet, while singing the song.

Display their work or use it for a bulletin board!

Here are the words sung to the tune of "Seven Steps."

Words by Debra Barger

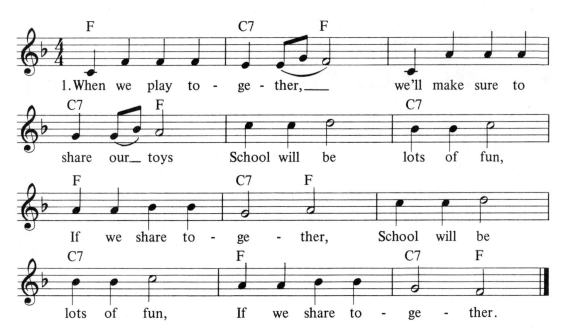

2. When we work together
   We'll make sure to listen well
   School would be lots of fun, If we work together,
   School would be lots of fun, If we work together.

Look what we can make!

Great group art projects are a natural way to encourage children to share materials and help one another. The arts and crafts and bulletin board ideas in this section have been successfully classroom tested with three-to six-year-olds. The fun-filled projects are easy to organize with easy-to-find materials. You'll love how the children work together to create colorful, imaginative room and bulletin board decorations.

A C T I V I T Y

Create a friend

BEHAVIORS: Cooperating, sharing

ACTIVITY: Art

MATERIALS: construction paper

scissors   crayons

glue   markers

DIRECTIONS: **1.** Draw a face shape on a piece of paper.

2. Cut out:

    a. different colors, lengths, and styles of hair from construction paper.

    b. different mouths (happy, sad, no expression).

    c. different shapes and expressions for eyes.

    d. different sizes and shapes of ears.

    e. beards, goatees, mustaches.

3. Group children in pairs or threes.
CONTINUED

4. Children can paste hair, nose, mouth, and other parts onto the face shape to create a friend.

5. Kids use crayons to draw a hat, earrings, and other accessories.

6. Let the children name their friends.

7. Hang the pictures of the new friends around the room.

8. Children may also cut out the picture and paste it on a stick to make a puppet and have their friend come alive for some puppetry.

Balloons over . . . (name of school)

BEHAVIOR: Comforting

ACTIVITY: Art

MATERIALS: paper balloons   variety of stickers

markers   poster board

12-inch pieces of multicolored ribbons

DIRECTIONS:

1. Cut out one paper balloon for each child in the group.

2. Let each child decorate his or her balloon with markers, stickers, and crayons.

3. If possible, the child writes his or her name on the balloon.

4. Attach a piece of multicolored ribbon to the balloon.

5. Glue all of the balloons to a large piece of poster board to resemble a bouquet of balloons.

6. Send the poster board balloon card to a sick friend.

—Beatrice Eaton

Handiwork quilt

BEHAVIORS: Cooperating, helping

ACTIVITY: Art

MATERIALS: different colors of finger paint

colored construction paper cut into 4-inch squares

DIRECTIONS: **1.** Give each child three 4-inch squares of construction paper. One is for a drawing and two are for handprints of each hand.

2. On one square, a child chooses a color of finger paint and draws a small picture of himself or herself.

3. The child covers his or her hands with paint and places the right hand on one of the other two squares and the left hand on the other.

4. Children write their names, if possible, on each of the three squares.

5. Arrange drawings and handprints on the bulletin board. Put a border on the outer edge of the squares.

6. Call one child to the board to find his or her handprints and tell whose handprints are next to his or hers. That person then tells whose prints are next to his or her prints. The two children hold hands. This is continued until all children are standing and holding hands.

—Deborah Cameron

The giving tree

BEHAVIORS: Comforting, helping

ACTIVITY: Art

MATERIALS:
coffee can   crayons

plaster of paris   water

tree branch   paint

paper leaves or other objects related to the season, such as Easter eggs or paper flowers

DIRECTIONS:

1. Mix the plaster of paris with water in the coffee can.

2. Place the tree branch in the can and allow it to set.

3. Let the children decorate the tree with cards made of paper leaves, paper Easter eggs, paper snow balls, or other objects according to the season.

4. To decorate, children color or paint their cards and write their names on them.

5. When a child, parent, or teacher is sick, the youngsters go to the tree and pick their card to send to the sick person.

—Beatrice Eaton

Community helpers bulletin board

BEHAVIORS: Cooperating, helping

ACTIVITY: Bulletin board

MATERIALS: paper cutouts of wheels, doors, windshields to construct a:
    fire engine   mail truck   police car

pictures of community helpers (firefighter, mail carrier, police officer)

glue

DIRECTIONS: 1. Divide the children into three groups. Each group is responsible for one of the following: police car, fire engine, mail truck.

2. Make the police car, fire engine, and mail truck by enlarging the patterns for your bulletin board.

3. Trace each part of the enlarged vehicle on different-colored construction paper to represent the actual color of the parts.

4. Cut out each part of the vehicle.

5. Give each group of children the enlarged pattern of a vehicle and cutout colored parts.

6. The groups of children glue each piece of the vehicle where it belongs— tires, emergency light, and doors.

7. Give the group a picture of a community helper and let them place it on the bulletin board in the appropriate place.

8. The fire truck and mail truck groups should follow similar directions for building their vehicles and placing them and their community helpers on the bulletin board.

—Beatrice Eaton

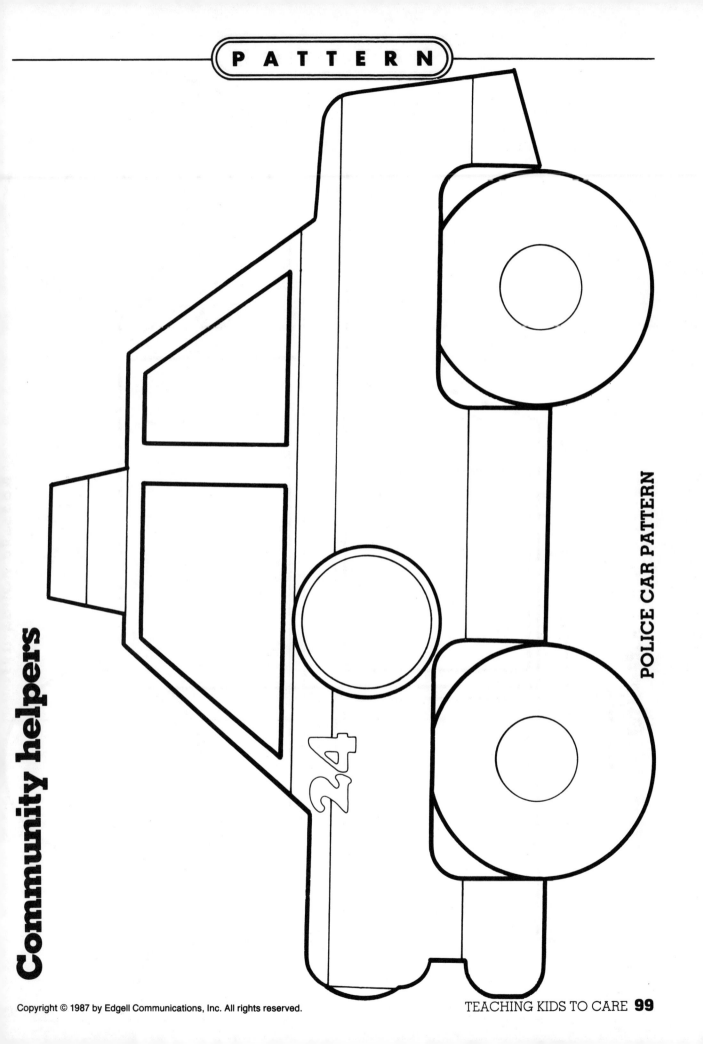

Community helpers

POLICE CAR PATTERN

24

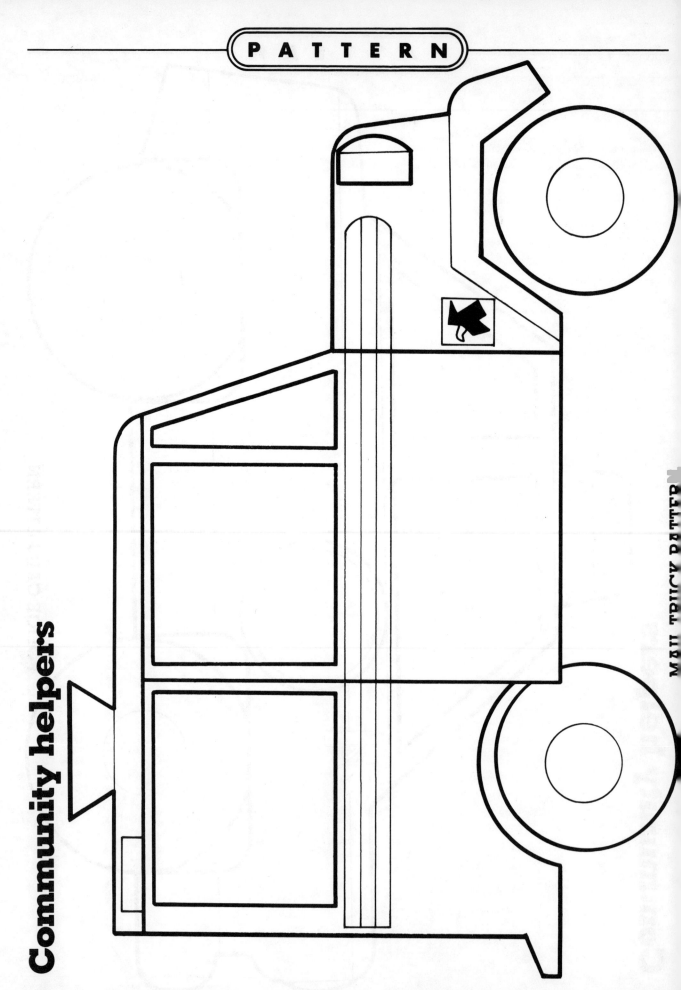

Community helpers

MAIL TRUCK PATTERN

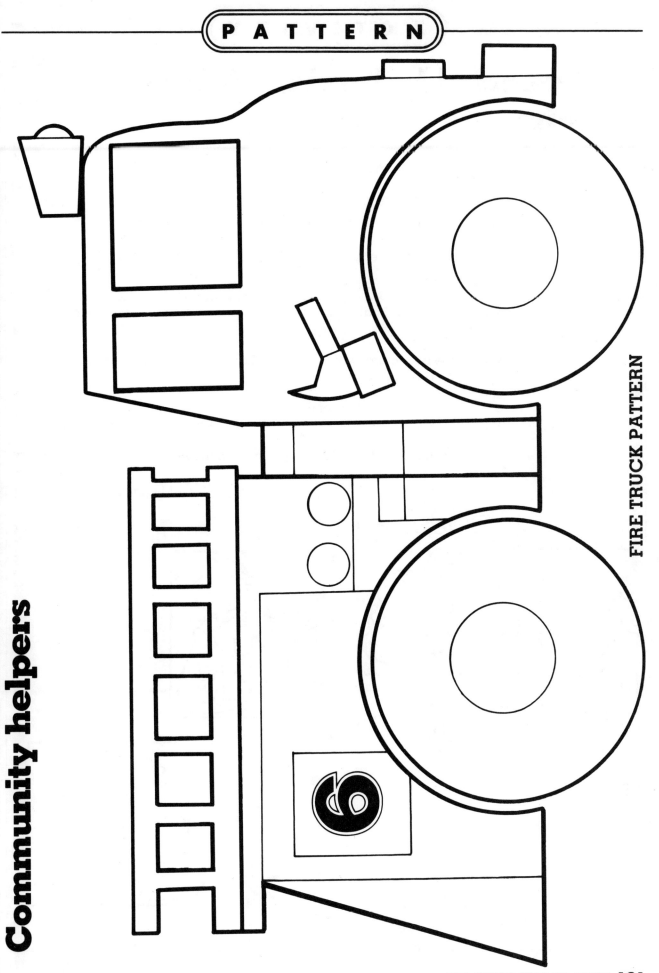

FIRE TRUCK PATTERN

Community helpers

Prosocial behavior of the hour

BEHAVIORS: Cooperating, helping (rescuing, defending, sharing, comforting)

ACTIVITY: Bulletin board/prosocial behaviors

MATERIALS: bulletin board

pictures of children engaging in prosocial behaviors (labeled)

poster board

DIRECTIONS: **1.** On a bulletin board, display a large paper clock with movable hands.

2. A labeled picture, which shows children engaged in prosocial behaviors, is placed at each hour.

3. As you turn the hands of the clock to each hour, encourage the group to discuss the particular behavior of the hour.

4. Practice and encourage the displayed behavior during the next hour.

—Margaret Bermens

Friendship tree

BEHAVIORS: Cooperating, helping

ACTIVITY: Bulletin board

MATERIALS: brown poster board or construction paper

picture of each child in the group

block letters

DIRECTIONS:

1. Make a tree trunk and tree branches from poster board or construction paper. You may wish to use a real tree branch.

2. Place the tree on the bulletin board.

3. Ask children to bring a picture of themselves from home.

4. Kids attach their pictures to a tree branch.

5. Place the heading "Friendship Tree" at the top in block letters.

FRIENDSHIP TREE

Holiday celebrations: a class affair

Holidays are a time to be jolly. They're a time to share the season with school friends and family. Planning new and exciting group activities to bring life and meaning to each holiday is not an easy task. In this section, we've planned happy activities for the entire class to work on and the whole school to enjoy. Share the fruits of your classes' labor by inviting parents and friends to see the festive spirit your class has created.

ACTIVITY

Five little jack o'lanterns

BEHAVIORS: Cooperating, helping

ACTIVITY: Finger play, art

MATERIALS:
finger play

crayons

dowel rods or rulers

stapler

newsprint cut into five
different large pumpkin shapes

orange construction paper cut
into pumpkin shapes

black construction paper cut
into eyes, nose, and mouth
shapes

shredded newspaper

DIRECTIONS: **1.** Let each child make his or her own jack o'lantern with the orange construction paper and eyes, noses, and mouths.

2. Tape dowel rods to the backs of the pumpkins.

3. Recite the finger play as a group a few times.

CONTINUED

4. Recite the finger play again, letting five different children use their puppets, each saying a part individually. Then do the play as a whole group.

5. For a Halloween decoration, children put the five jack o'lanterns on a gate.

> a. Let kids choose partners.
>
> b. Give partners the same pumpkin pattern cut from newsprint. (See following page.)
>
> c. The children can then color their jack o'lanterns with crayons.
>
> d. Staple edges of the partners' pumpkins together, leaving an opening for stuffing.
>
> e. Kids stuff the pumpkins with newspaper. Staple the opening shut.
>
> f. They color some paper brown and you cut it into gate planks.
>
> g. Tape gate planks to the edge of a table and put the jack o'lanterns on the table.

FINGER PLAY: "FIVE LITTLE JACK O'LANTERNS"

Five little jack o'lanterns sitting on a gate;
The first one said, "My, it's getting late."
The second one said, "I hear a noise."
The third one said, "It's just a lot of boys."
The fourth one said, "Come on let's run."
The fifth one said, "It's just Halloween fun!"

Poof! went the wind and out went the lights
And away ran the jack o'lanterns on Halloween night.

—Deborah Cameron

Jack o'lantern patterns

Stand-up balloon jack o'lanterns

BEHAVIORS: Cooperating, sharing

ACTIVITY: Holiday art, creative dramatics

MATERIALS: stand-up balloons (orange or black)   glue
patterns of jack o'lantern parts

DIRECTIONS: **1.** Cut out various jack o'lantern face and body parts from the patterns.

2. Blow up balloons and place them on their feet.

3. Let children decorate their balloon jack o'lanterns by gluing on the parts.

4. Each child describes his or her jack o'lantern and what it says and does.

5. Work with the kids to develop a short skit using their jack o'lantern balloons.

6. Let them put on the skit for another group.

Jack o'lantern outfits

Shape up for Halloween

BEHAVIORS: Cooperating, sharing, helping

ACTIVITY: Halloween—bulletin board or collage wall hanging

MATERIALS: black, white, yellow construction paper

patterns for different-sized circles, triangles, rectangles, and half-circles

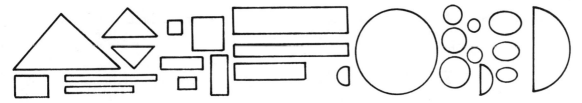

DIRECTIONS:

1. Make a sample bat, witch, and cat for the kids to use as patterns.

2. Depending upon the age of the children, you or the children can trace and cut out many different shapes from the black construction paper.

3. Trace and cut out a few white circles for a witch's face.

4. Trace and cut out different-sized rectangles in yellow for the witch's hair, witch's broom, and the cat's eyes and whiskers.

5. Divide the youngsters into four groups.

6. Make each group responsible for creating two bats, a witch, and a cat using the different shapes and following the basic patterns. Encourage the children to use their imagination.

7. You place large shapes on the bulletin board or collage paper to make a house.

8. Each group places its cats, bats, and witches around the house to create a Halloween scene.

Pumpkin power

BEHAVIORS: Cooperating, sharing

ACTIVITY: Halloween art

MATERIALS: several medicine droppers   orange paint   glue

9″ x 12″ white construction paper

yellow and black construction paper

DIRECTIONS:

1. Give each child one sheet of paper. Fold the 9″ x 12″ white construction paper in half, then open the paper flat. Have kids do the same.

2. Each child drops orange paint onto one-half of the paper with a medicine dropper.

3. Immediately fold the paper and rub a hand over the folded paper. Open the paper and allow the paint to dry.

4. When the paper is dry, give the children a pumpkin shape to trace and cut out of the blotted paper. If the children are old enough, they may wish to draw their own pumpkin shapes.

5. The children can glue eyes, mouth, and nose cut from yellow or black construction paper onto the pumpkin. The eyes, nose, and mouth can be made from cutting construction paper into various shapes.

6. Have each child take his or her pumpkin to another classroom, group room, or director's office to hang on the door or decorate a wall.

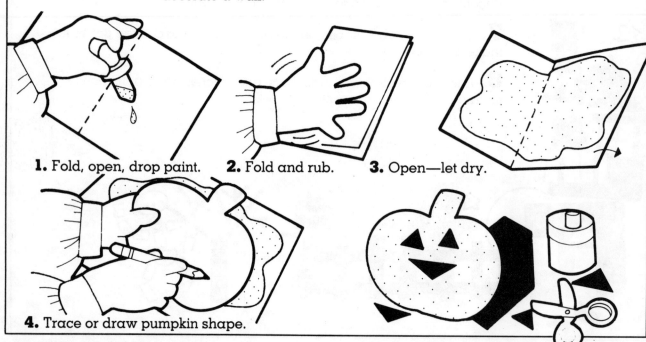

1. Fold, open, drop paint.   **2.** Fold and rub.   **3.** Open—let dry.

4. Trace or draw pumpkin shape.

Haunted classroom

BEHAVIORS: Cooperating, sharing, helping

ACTIVITY: Halloween art

MATERIALS: paper plates

black and yellow construction paper

a variety of fluorescent paints

glue

DIRECTIONS: **1.** Divide the children into three groups.

2. One group makes paper plate spiders (see pattern). Paint the body of the spider (paper plate) with fluorescent paint.

3. Group two makes witches from black construction paper (see pattern). Paint the witches with fluorescent paint.

4. Group three makes bats from black construction paper (see pattern). Paint the bats with fluorescent paint.

5. Hang the bats, witches, and spiders from the ceiling using different lengths of yarn.

6. Invite other classes to visit your Haunted Classroom.

7. When they arrive, turn the lights off, play some spooky Halloween music, and use a fan or have the children wave pieces of construction paper to make the bats, witches, and spiders "fly" around the room.

NOTE: Teachers should not bring very young children to visit your classroom because it might frighten them too much. Older youngsters who visit should also be prepared for what they will see so they will not be frightened.

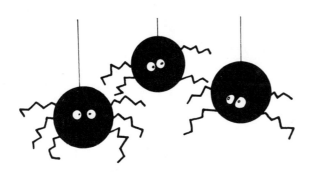

Spiders

Make the legs with eight strips of black construction paper folded like a fan.

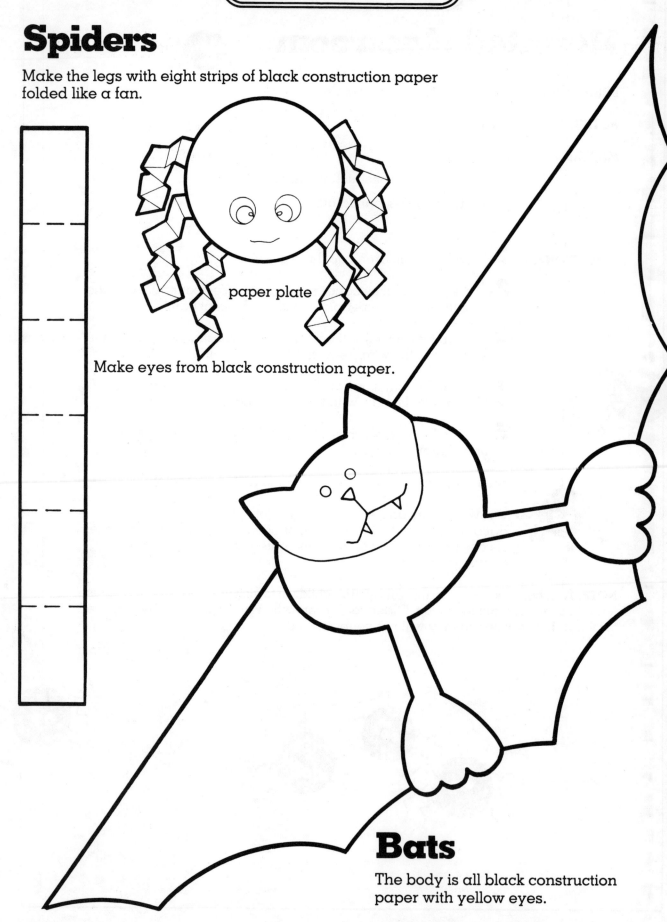

paper plate

Make eyes from black construction paper.

Bats

The body is all black construction paper with yellow eyes.

Witch

Black cat

Gobble, gobble/Thanksgiving

BEHAVIOR: Cooperating

ACTIVITY: Thanksgiving art, bulletin board

MATERIALS: finger paint (fall colors)   finger painting paper
turkey body and head

DIRECTIONS: **1.** Place the turkey body and head on the bulletin board with the heading "Gobble, Gobble."

2. Let children finger paint freely on a piece of finger painting paper.

3. When dry, trace a feather out of the painting, and let the children cut it out.

4. If they can, children write their names on the backs of the feathers, and mix the feathers up. Kids first find and then attach their feathers to the turkey to create a tail of many colors.

—Beatrice Eaton

GOBBLE, GOBBLE

Five little turkeys

BEHAVIORS: Cooperating, sharing, helping

ACTIVITY: Finger play

MATERIALS: none

DIRECTIONS: Read the following finger play and do the actions with the youngsters. Do it enough times so everyone can do one part individually.

Five little turkeys hard at play (show five fingers)
Getting ready for Thanksgiving Day.
The first one said, "I'll set the table" (pantomime setting the table).
The second one said, "I'll help if I am able" (point to self).
The third one said, "Let's make pumpkin pie!" (stirring motions).
The fourth one said, "Together, let's try!" (point to self, then other).
The fifth one said, "Our feast is done; together we've helped to make our work fun!" (point to everyone).

—Margaret Bermens

Potato latke feast

BEHAVIORS: Cooperating, sharing, helping

ACTIVITY: Holiday—Hanukkah

MATERIALS: Potato latke recipe

Ingredients: 10 potatoes, 5 onions, 5 eggs, 2 cups of flour, salt to taste, oil for frying.

Applesauce, sour cream, pineapple sauce, any kind of canned berries.

DIRECTIONS:

1. First the children wash the potatoes and dry them.

2. Place the potatoes, onions, eggs, flour, and salt in a food processor or blender.

3. Drop the mixture by large spoonfuls into hot oil in a frying pan. (Make sure the children are far enough away not to get splashed with the hot oil.) Fry until they are cooked. Drain them on a paper towel.

4. Place applesauce, sour cream, pineapple sauce, and berries in individual containers with a spoon.

5. Invite another class or group to enjoy the feast with your kids.

6. Give each child a plate with a latke and a fork or spoon. Each child spoons one or several of his or her favorite toppings on the latkes.

A C T I V I T Y

Hanukkah fun

BEHAVIORS: Cooperating, sharing, helping

ACTIVITY: Holiday—Hanukkah

MATERIALS: Hanukkah dreidel ('dra dle) or

four-inch square of construction paper, marker, pencil

DIRECTIONS: 1. To make a Hanukkah dreidel, put a dot at the center of a four-inch square of construction paper, and fold each corner to meet the center dot. Turn paper over so folds are underneath, and write one of these Hebrew letters along each edge:

Nun ‫נ‬   Gimel ‫ג‬   Hey ‫ה‬   Shin ‫ש‬

Insert a pencil through the dot and you are ready to spin.

2. If you feel your class is old enough, or if you would like to send directions home for the dreidel game, here's how to play. Each player is given the same number of playing items, for instance pennies or candies. Before play begins, each player contributes one item to the middle. Players take turns spinning the dreidel. If the spin ends on <u>nun</u>, the player receives nothing from the middle and puts nothing in; <u>gimel</u>, the player takes everything from the pot; <u>hey</u>, the player takes half; and <u>shin</u>, the player has to put something in.

3. Teach children the following Hanukkah song, sung to the tune of "Twinkle, Twinkle, Little Star."

Song: Dreidel, dreidel spinning strong,
Hanukkah is eight days long.
Candles, candles burning bright,
Light one more on every night.
Laughing, singing, presents, too,
Happy Hanukkah to you!

Friendship wreath/Christmas

BEHAVIORS: Cooperating, sharing

ACTIVITY: Holidays

MATERIALS: green and red construction paper

crayons   scissors   stapler   glue

DIRECTIONS:

1. Group children into pairs.

2. Each child draws his or her partner's hands—one on green paper and the other on red.

3. Depending on their ages, the children may cut out the paper tracings of their own hands.

4. Cut a ring from red or green paper, with the outside diameter 8" and the inside diameter 6".

5. Each child takes a turn stapling or gluing the cutouts of his or her hands onto the ring.

6. A bow may be added for decoration.

7. Hang the wreath on the school or classroom door.

—Deborah Cameron

RED

GREEN

Tree-trimming party

BEHAVIORS: Cooperating, sharing

ACTIVITY: Holiday—bulletin board, wall hanging, door decoration

MATERIALS:

green construction paper	white paper
aluminum foil	markers
different-colored curled ribbon pieces	glue
multicolored construction paper	treats
short pieces of garland	
sheets of cotton or cotton balls	

DIRECTIONS:

1. Make a large Christmas tree from the green construction paper to hang on the bulletin board or wall.

CONTINUED

2. Tell the kids to use their imagination and decorate the tree by gluing any of the various materials they choose on the tree.

3. Show them how to glue cotton balls under the tree for a skirt.

4. Pull cotton apart and glue around the tree for snowflakes.

5. Cut multicolored construction paper into various sizes to represent presents.

6. Children "decorate" the Christmas presents and place them under the tree.

Deck the halls

BEHAVIORS: Cooperating, sharing (information and materials)

ACTIVITY: Holiday—Christmas

MATERIALS: depends on the project

DIRECTIONS: **1.** Let your group decide which school hall they would like to decorate for Christmas.

2. Have the kids decide the theme. For example, they might choose an outside winter scene with Santa Claus, elves, and a sleigh traveling through the sky.

3. Draw a picture of the scene to see if the group wants to change anything.

4. Encourage the group to be creative in deciding what materials they will need.

5. Work with the children to gather all of the materials.

6. Make any pattern you will need.

7. Now "Deck the Halls!"

Heart-to-heart/Valentine's Day

BEHAVIOR: Cooperation

ACTIVITY: Holiday—word recognition, bulletin board

MATERIALS: red poster board

white and pink construction paper

marker

DIRECTIONS: **1.** Cut out a large red poster board heart and attach it to the wall or bulletin board.

2. Cut out small hearts from pink and white construction paper.

3. Each morning during circle time, ask the children to think of Valentine words that begin with certain sounds.

4. Write each word on a heart.

5. Have one child pin the small hearts around the large heart to make an attractive group Valentine bulletin board.

Heart piñatas

BEHAVIORS: Cooperating, sharing (information and materials)

ACTIVITY: Holiday—word recognition

MATERIALS: red poster board

                  white construction paper cut into small hearts

                  red magic marker

                  string

                  paper punch

DIRECTIONS:

1. Make different sized heart shapes for half the number of children in your group. Now make a second set of hearts that match the first set.

2. Each child picks out one of the heart shapes.

3. Each youngster finds a "buddy." This is his or her classmate who has the same size heart shape.

4. Staple the "buddies'" hearts together, leaving a space at the top.

5. The "buddies" fill their heart with Valentine words which you have previously written on small white construction paper hearts.

6. Next, they lace a string through their heart and hang it from the ceiling.

7. Each child gets a chance to break his or her heart piñata.

8. The "buddies" pick up their Valentine words and read them to each other.

Responsibilities and rewards

Two more Rs in the early childhood curriculum are assigning responsibilities and giving rewards. Children love to have special classroom jobs to help the teacher and their friends. Assign at least two children to each task so they can share responsibilities. Giving group rewards for positive prosocial behavior reduces individual competition and increases the occurrence of the appropriate behavior. This section contains motivating suggestions for assigning classroom jobs and exciting group charts for giving rewards and reinforcing prosocial behaviors. You'll find the young children working hard to learn their jobs and earn their rewards.

BADGES

"I PUT SCISSORS AWAY"

'I'M A CLEANER TODAY"

"I PASS OUT THE SNACKS"

"I PASS OUT SUPPLIES"

I'M A GOOD FRIEND

I AM KIND TO OTHERS

I LOVE TO HELP

I LOVE
TO SHARE

Recipes for group fun

Cooking up something special in the early childhood program enhances a cooperative, helpful atmosphere. Children join together to mix, stir, chop, bake, and, of course, sample as they go along. When everything is prepared, there is still the group job of cleaning up. Planning and organizing are the keys to a successful group cooking project. In this chapter, you'll find some mouth-watering, interesting, and fun ideas for your class. The recipes are easy-to-follow and inexpensive to make. Have the children wash their hands so the treats can be finger-lickin' good!

ACTIVITY

Punch party

BEHAVIORS: Cooperating, sharing

ACTIVITY: Cooking—snack

MATERIALS:
ginger ale	ladle
orange juice	long spoon
apple juice	cups
cherries	punch bowl
oranges	

DIRECTIONS:

1. Place all ingredients on the table.

2. Ask different children to pour in different ingredients and stir the mixture.

3. When finished, children take turns ladling some into their cups and enjoy the fruits of their labor!

ACTIVITY

Build a snack

BEHAVIORS: Cooperating, sharing

ACTIVITY: Cooking

MATERIALS:
bread	cream cheese	banana slices
peanut butter	plastic knives	chopped nuts
raisins		

DIRECTIONS:

1. Group four children together.

2. Give each group:

two slices of bread

one plastic knife

small cups filled with snack fixings (raisins, peanut butter, nuts, and so on).

3. Each group builds a sandwich snack.

4. Cut the sandwich into four pieces.

5. Each child is allowed to eat a quarter of the sandwich for a snack.

NOTE: Make sure that no child is allergic to any of the snack fixings. If so, supply an alternative.

ACTIVITY

A thankful feast

BEHAVIORS: Cooperating, sharing (materials and information)

ACTIVITY: Cooking—Thanksgiving

MATERIALS:

popcorn	pumpkin cookies
napkins	paper plates
drink mix	pitcher

DIRECTIONS:

1. Read a book about the first Thanksgiving.

2. Divide the children into three groups.

3. Give each group a job to prepare for their own "first" Thanksgiving feast. For example, one group could set the table, another group might distribute food, and a third group could serve the drink.

4. After the table is set and the food and drink served, the children eat their "first Thanksgiving feast."

—Margaret Bermens

A C T I V I T Y

Summer birthdays

BEHAVIORS: Cooperating, sharing (materials and information)

ACTIVITY: Cooking, celebrations

MATERIALS:
crêpe paper   spoon   bowl

tape   baking pan

balloons   cake mix

DIRECTIONS:

1. Tell the children that they are going to celebrate all of the summer birthdays of the kids in the class.

2. Divide the children into two groups.

3. With your help, the first group mixes and stirs ingredients to make a cake.

4. Give the second group balloons, crêpe paper, and tape to decorate the classroom for a party.

5. When each group completes its task, it is time to celebrate the birthdays of all the children who have birthdays during the summer!

6. Make sure that all children work together to clean up.

—Margaret Bermens

PART III

Parents as partners in prosocial development

Make parents part of your prosocial program. Children tend to act prosocially when they observe cooperation and helpfulness at home. Since parents are important allies in prosocial development, you need to enlist their help. In this chapter, you'll find a ready-to-duplicate letter to parents explaining your prosocial development goals and encouraging their cooperation. Send this letter home at the beginning of the school year. The remainder of the chapter contains nine monthly send-home activity sheets, from September through May, with loads of useful suggestions, clever time-saving tips, and enjoyable prosocial activities.

Dear Parent:

Something special is happening in our classroom this year and we need your help! Throughout the year, your child will be participating in many exciting, challenging activities and situations to help him or her learn to cooperate with and help others. Cooperating and helping behaviors are called prosocial behavior.

What can you do to help your child learn and practice these behaviors? As a parent, you can do a great deal at home to reinforce prosocial behavior. You can model these behaviors for your child. When your child sees you cooperating with, sharing with, comforting, and helping family, friends, neighbors, and others, he or she is likely to act in a similar manner.

At the beginning of each month, your child will bring home a prosocial activity sheet with useful suggestions, clever tips, and fun-filled activities for working and playing together as a family. Keep in mind that the time you and your child spend on these activities should be a happy, pleasant, relaxing time—a time for talking, laughing, sharing, cooperating, and helping. Remember that the purpose of these send-home sheets is to work together as a family. If the project does not turn out perfectly, do not be concerned. You did accomplish the goal—that is, you reinforced prosocial behavior at home.

So look for these activity sheets. And please do not forget to read them carefully and try the ideas. It is important to your child's total development.

Sincerely yours,

_____

Badges for home activities

When you and your child have successfully completed some of the prosocial activities, here's a fun reward for a project well done. Make prosocial badges from poster board or felt with such appropriate messages as "We work together," "We enjoy helping each other," and "I like to comfort my family." Then let your child decorate the badges with glue, sequins, yarn, buttons, or any other objects available at home. Perhaps he or she could decorate the badges seasonally—an apple for fall, a snowflake for winter, a flower for spring, and the sun for summer.

WE ENJOY HELPING EACH OTHER

I LOVE MY FAMILY

WE WORK TOGETHER

I LIKE TO COMFORT MY FAMILY

SEPTEMBER:
Fall into step

Dear Parent,

Fall is an ideal time for families to share the wonders of nature. Here are autumn activities that you can do at home to practice and reinforce the prosocial behaviors like cooperating and helping that we have been learning in school. Have fun!

Fall Read-Alouds: Stop by your library or bookstore and choose a few of these autumn favorites the whole family will enjoy.

Autumn Harvest. Alvin R. Tresselt.
Follow the Fall. Maxine W. Kumin.
It's Autumn. Naomi Weygant.
Mice Came in Early This Year, The. Eleanor J. Lapp.
Now It's Fall. Lois L. Lenski.
Peter Pumpkin. John Ott and Pete Coley.
Tale of Squirrel Nutkin, The. Beatrix Potter.

Family Fun: Gather the family together for a walk outdoors. Look for signs of the changing season, such as leaves turning colors or the sun setting earlier in the day. Share your knowledge of nature with your child and explore together.

On another day, head for the park or your own backyard. Work together to gather leaves into a pile. Your child will enjoy running and jumping into the leaves. If you're feeling young at heart, give it a try!

An Experience to Remember: After your walk or after playing in the leaves ask your child to tell you what you saw and did and what he or she liked best. Print everything on a piece of paper. Read it to your child, then ask him or her read it to you.

OCTOBER:
Bewitching prosocial fun

Dear Parent,

October is the time of year for families to work together to create a Halloween spirit in the home. Remember, your child is working hard at school to learn to cooperate, help, share with, and comfort others. Here are Halloween activities that will get the whole family involved.

Halloween Books: Visit the library or bookstore to get these Halloween favorites.

Everyone Goes as a Pumpkin by Judith Vigna. Chicago: Albert Whitman, 1977.
Halloween Party by Lonzo Anderson. New York: Macmillan, 1974.
It's Halloween by Jack Prelutsky. New York: Greenwillow, 1977.
Space Witch by Don Freeman. New York: Penguin, 1979.
A Woggle of Witches by Adrienne Adams. New York: Macmillan, 1971.

The following books are out of print. However, you may still find them at your school or public library, and they are still good resources:

Let's Catch a Monster by Ann Herbert Scott.
The Pumpkin Giant by Ellin Greene.
Sir Halloween by Jerrold Beim.

Delightful Decorations: Make some Halloween decorations as a family. Decide where to place them. Also use the decorations your child makes at school. Here are a few other easy, fun-to-make decorations you may want to try:
●**Paper Pumpkins:** Cut different pumpkin shapes from orange construction paper. Have each family member make a jack o' lantern face with a black marker.
●**Ghosts:** Place a tissue over a lollipop. Tie a piece of black yarn at the base of the lollipop to make the ghost's neck. Use black marker to make a face.
●**Spiders:** Cut two black pipe cleaners into eight pieces. Buy black licorice gumdrops. Insert four pipe cleaner spider legs on each side of a gumdrop.

Festive Feast: On Halloween night let your children decorate your tablecloth with paper pumpkins or Halloween stickers. Place the lighted jack o'lantern on the table as a centerpiece. Turn the lights down or off. For your dinner drink have the family make a witches brew:

orange juice
apple juice
pineapple juice
maraschino cherries

Place liquids into a pot, stir, then ladle into cups at the table.

Create a Costume: Talk with your children about a Halloween costume. Using everyone's ideas, draw a picture of the costume. Work together to list all of the items needed for the costume. Take a bag on a scavenger hunt for the needed items for the costume. Make or buy the parts you don't have.

NOVEMBER:
Thanks, turkey, and trimmings

Dear Parent,

November, a month for giving thanks, is a wonderful time for cooperating with and helping family and nonfamily members. Here are some ideas to help you reinforce prosocial behavior while creating a warm, giving atmosphere in your home.

Gobbling-Good Books: Don't forget to stop by the library or bookstore to get a few of these Thanksgiving favorites:

Cranberry Thanksgiving by Wende Devlin and Harry Devlin. New York: Macmillan, 1980.

Little Bear's Thanksgiving by Janice Brustlein. New York: Lothrop, Lee & Shepard, 1967.

Over the River and Through the Wood by Lydia Maria Child. New York: Putnam Publishing Group, 1974.

Sometimes It's Turkey—Sometimes It's Feathers by Lorna Balian. Nashville, Tenn.: Abingdon Press, 1973.

The Thanksgiving Story by Alice Dalgliesh. New York: Macmillan, 1985.

The Giving Bag: Decorate a paper bag with a picture of a turkey cut from a newspaper or magazine; add labels from various canned goods. Throughout the month, fill the bag with canned and packaged foods to share with and comfort a less fortunate family. Look in your local newspaper for agencies or organizations that distribute food. Take your giving bag on a day when the entire family can go. Encourage your kids to ask questions when you go to the organization.

Thanksgiving Picture Menu: Have your family prepare a Thanksgiving menu by looking through magazines that contain pictures of food. When each member finds something special to eat, he or she cuts out the picture. All pictures are sorted and organized into food groups. On each page of the menu glue pictures of one of the kinds of foods. For example: meat, vegetables, desserts, potatoes/breads, soups.

Feather Fun: Cut turkey feathers from any kind of paper you have handy. On each feather write a responsibility: set table, pick up toys, rock the baby, collect garbage, share toys. In the morning, have each member of the family choose a feather. That person's job for the day (or week) is written on the feather.

TAKE•HOME

DECEMBER:
Prosocial bright ideas

Dear Parent,

Light up your December with some bright ideas to encourage cooperating and helping behaviors in your family. Celebrate the joys you'll discover working and playing together at this festive time of year.

Festive Books: Brighten up each day by reading one of these Christmas or Hanukkah stories. They will get your family into the spirit of the season.

CHRISTMAS

The Christmas Mouse by Elizabeth Wenning. New York: Holt, 1959.
The Little Drummer Boy by Ezra Jack Keats. New York: Macmillan, 1972.
The Little Fir Tree by Margaret Wise Brown. New York: Crowell, 1985.
The Mole Family's Christmas by Russell Conwell Hoban. New York: Scholastic, 1982.
The Nicest Gift by Leo Politi. New York: Scribner, 1973.
The Night Before Christmas by Clement Clarke Moore. New York: Simon & Schuster, 1986.
Santa's Moose by Sydney Hoff. New York: Harper & Row Junior Books, 1979.
Where's Prancer? by Sydney Hoff. New York: Harper & Row Junior Books, 1969.

HANUKKAH

A Picture Book of Hanukkah by David A. Adler. New York: Holiday House, 1982.
Chanukah by Norma Simon. New York: Crowell, 1966.
It's Chanukah! by Ellie Gellman. Rockville, Md.: Kar-Ben Copies, 1985.
Light Another Candle: The Story and Meaning of Hanukkah by Miriam Chaikin. New York: Clarion, 1981.
My Very Own Chanukah Book by Judyth Saypol and Madeline Wikler. Rockville, Md.: Kar-Ben Copies, 1977.

Hanukkah Fun: Let your whole family participate in a special cooking project. The result—traditional latkes, or potato pancakes. Try this recipe, and enjoy!

10 potatoes	2 cups flour
5 onions	salt to taste
5 eggs	oil for frying

Mix together in a food processor or blender. Make into pancake shapes and fry.

Tree-mendous Trimmings: Trim your Christmas tree with a few of these decorations made by the family.
Loops: String Fruitloops on pieces of yarn. Tie the yarn to make a variety of loops.
Circles: Cut circles from construction paper, cover them with glue, and add sparkles. Punch holes at the top and lace them with yarn.
Stars: Cut a star from green, red, yellow, or blue felt. Paste a picture of each member of the family in the center of the star. Use alphabet macaroni to spell each member's name. Use craft glue to put the name under the picture.

JANUARY:
New year novelties

Dear Parent,

Ring in the new year with some family fun. Warm up to each other with wintertime books, then plan your yearly calendar and monthly resolutions, and, finally, make some frosty treats and learn about the Chinese New Year celebration.

Winter-Wonderful Books: Look for a few of these books at your library or bookstore to warm up your January.

<u>In a Meadow, Two Hares Ride</u> by Jennifer Bartoli. Chicago: Albert Whitman, 1978.
<u>The Snowy Day</u> by Ezra Jack Keats. New York: Viking, 1962.
<u>When Will It Snow?</u> by Sydney Hoff. New York: Harper Junior Books, 1971.

The following books are no longer in print. However, you may still find them in your local library and they are still good resources.

<u>All Ready for Winter</u> by Leone Adelson.
<u>City in the Winter</u> by Eleanor Schick.
<u>I Like Winter</u> by Lois Lenski.
<u>Little Bear's New Year's Party</u> by Janice Brustlein.
<u>Winter's Coming</u> by Eve Bunting.

Personalized Calendar: Take down the old calendar in your home. Before putting up a new one, go through each month of the year with your child and mark the family's special days—birthdays, school or family vacations, and dates to remember. Your child may use stickers or circle the date.

Resolutions-by-the-Month: At the beginning of each month, sit down as a family and decide on some resolutions for the month. Write the resolutions down on the calendar. At the end of the month, have the family decide whether everyone was successful in carrying them out.

Frozen Fruits: When the temperature falls below freezing, put some grapes or banana slices in a freezer bag. Put the bag outside. When the fruit freezes, take it inside and enjoy a refreshing, healthy, icy treat.

Chinese New Year: Celebrate the Chinese New Year on the appropriate date in January (it changes yearly) with children's stories and Chinese traditions.

TRADITIONS

1. Give your children bright red envelopes with good luck wishes inside.
2. The dragon is the symbol of strength and good luck used to celebrate the new year. Decorate your front door with this good luck symbol.

FEBRUARY:
February fantasies

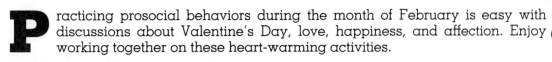

Dear Parent,

Practicing prosocial behaviors during the month of February is easy with discussions about Valentine's Day, love, happiness, and affection. Enjoy working together on these heart-warming activities.

Valentine Books: The library is filled with books to share with your child throughout the month. Here are a few good ones.

Bee My Valentine by Miriam Cohen. New York: Greenwillow, 1978.
Little Love Story by Fernando Krahn. New York: Lippincott Junior Books, 1976.
Washington's Birthday by Clyde Robert Bulla. New York: Crowell Junior Books, 1967.

The following books are no longer in print. However, you may still find them at your public library. They are still very good resources.

The Hunt for Rabbit's Galosh by Ann Schweninger.
She Loves Me, She Loves Me Not by Robert Keeshan.

Heavenly Heart (Pot) Holders:

1. Gather together some red, white, and pink yarn, glue, and a sheet of waxed paper.
2. Pour glue into a Styrofoam or foil pie pan, adding a small amount of water.
3. Cut long pieces of yarn.
4. Dip the pieces of yarn into the glue. Make sure the yarn is saturated.
5. Draw a heart shape on the waxed paper.
6. Lay the glue-dipped yarn in the heart outline.
7. Continue to lay yarn pieces until the entire heart shape is filled.
8. Let it dry overnight.
9. In the morning pull the heart from the waxed paper.

Groundhog Shadow Play:
In a dark room, turn a flashlight on a blank wall. Have everyone try to make groundhogs on the wall with their hands. It is also fun to make other shadow animals.

Newsworthy Hats (George Washington Hats):

1. Fold a large sheet of newspaper at prefolded line.
2. Work with the folded edge at the top.
3. Fold top left corner into the center of the page.
4. Fold the top right corner into the center of the page.
5. Fold the remaining paper at the bottom of one side up.
6. Turn over and fold paper at bottom of other edge up.
7. Staple or tape seam and flaps.

TAKE•HOME

MARCH:

Spring forth with prosocial behavior

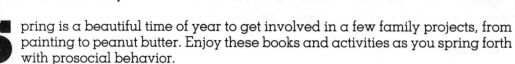

Dear Parent,

Spring is a beautiful time of year to get involved in a few family projects, from painting to peanut butter. Enjoy these books and activities as you spring forth with prosocial behavior.

Springtime Books: Here are some wonderful books about spring to share with your family.

The Happy Day by Ruth Krauss. New York: Harper Junior Books, 1949.
The Hungry Leprechaun by Mary Calhoun. New York: William Morrow, 1962.
Little Bear Marches in the St. Patrick's Day Parade by Janice Brustlein. New York: Lothrop, Lee & Shepard.
Spring Is Here! by Jane B. Moncure. Chicago: Children's Press, 1975.
The Sugar Snow Spring by Lillian Hoban. New York: Harper Junior Books, 1973.

The following books are no longer in print. However, you may still find them at your public library. They are good resources.

Hi, Mr. Robin by Alvin Tresselt.
It's Spring by Noemi Weygant.
One Bright Monday Morning by Arline Baum and Joseph Baum.
What Happens in the Spring by Kathleen Costello Beer.

String Time (Wind Chimes):

1. Put two small holes in the middle of an aluminum pie pan. Make six holes around the outer edge of the pie pan.

2. Tie nails, tin cans, or shells to the ends of six pieces of string.

3. Knot the strings through the holes on the outer edge of the pie pan so that the nails, tin cans, or shells are hanging down.

4. Knot one piece of string through the middle hole to hang the wind chime outside.

Home Cleanup Day: Don't put off your spring cleaning any longer. Gather the troops together to tackle a really big job such as the attic, garage, basement, or playroom. Have two garbage bags ready—one for trash and one for giveaways.

140 TEACHING KIDS TO CARE

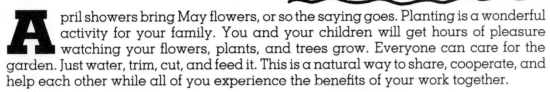

APRIL:
Fresh start

Dear Parent,

April showers bring May flowers, or so the saying goes. Planting is a wonderful activity for your family. You and your children will get hours of pleasure watching your flowers, plants, and trees grow. Everyone can care for the garden. Just water, trim, cut, and feed it. This is a natural way to share, cooperate, and help each other while all of you experience the benefits of your work together.

A Shower of Books: Books about Easter, the weather, and flowers.

Dandelion by Don Freeman. New York: Viking, 1964.
The Easter Egg Artists by Adrienne Adams. New York: Macmillan, 1976.
Easter Treat by Roger Antoine Duvoisin. New York: Knopf, 1954.
The Gunniwolf retold by Wilhelmina Harper. New York: Dutton, 1967.
A Letter to Amy by Ezra Jack Keats. New York: Harper Junior Books, 1984.
My Red Umbrella by Robert Bright. New York: William Morrow, 1985.

The following books are no longer in print. However, they are still good resources and you might find them in your local library.

The Adventures of Egbert the Easter Egg by Richard Willard Armour.
Aunt Bella's Umbrella by William Cole.
Barney Bipple's Magic Dandelions by Carol Chapman.
Daddy Long Ears by Robert Kraus.
The Golden Egg Book by Margaret Wise Brown.
The Good Rain by Alice E. Goudey.
The King's Flower by Mitsumasa Anno.
The World in the Candy Egg by Alvin R. Tresselt.

Egg Plants! Have your family plant marigold seeds in half of a broken eggshell. Place the shells back in the egg carton. Place the egg carton on a sunny windowsill. When they are strong enough, choose a special place outside for everyone to transplant his or her marigolds. Watch the seedlings grow into flowers.

Flower Power Treat: Include your child in the preparation of two delicious fun-to-make recipes.
1. Cut up raw or slightly cooked broccoli and cauliflower. Make a dip from your favorite dry salad dressing mix and plain yogurt. Enjoy this healthy snack!
2. Your child will love to eat this bunny salad. Place half a pear on a piece of a lettuce. Have your child decorate the pears by adding two raisins for eyes, a cinnamon candy for the nose, a marshmallow for the tail, and almond halves for ears.

Plant Salad: Have a brief discussion of the parts of a plant using salad fixings. Ask the kids for examples of other vegetables and help them understand which part of a plant it is.

Anatomy of a Plant

Flower—Cauliflower	Roots—Carrot	Stem—Celery
Leaf—Lettuce	Fruit—Apple	

Cut everything up in a bowl and add your favorite dressing.

MAY:
May days

Dear Parent,

The school year is coming to a close. We have had wonderful experiences learning and practicing our prosocial behaviors. Thank you for cooperating with and helping your child learn these important behaviors. Next month, you'll receive an activity sheet for the summer months. Until then, enjoy these May activities and books at your house.

May Books:
Anno's Journey by Mitsumasa Anno. New York: Putnam Publishing Group, 1981.
Dreams by Peter Spier. New York: Doubleday, 1986.
Read Aloud Rhymes for the Very Young, ed. by Jack Prelutsky. New York: Knopf, 1986.
Sunshine by Jan Ormerod. New York: Lothrop, Lee & Shepard, 1981.
The Surprise by George Shannon. New York: Greenwillow, 1983.
The Very Hungry Caterpillar by Eric Carle. New York: Putnam Publishing Group, 1981.

May Flowers for Someone Special: Cut out the little Vs in between the plastic egg cartons. Fill the V with clay or Play-do. Place silk, plastic, or dried flowers in the clay or Play-do. Give them to mom, grandma, aunt, or some special person.

May Day: Place a long stick or pole in the ground outside. Attach crêpe paper strips from the top of the stick or pole with a heavy-duty tape. On May Day (May 1), have your family and friends hold on to a streamer and dance around the May pole.

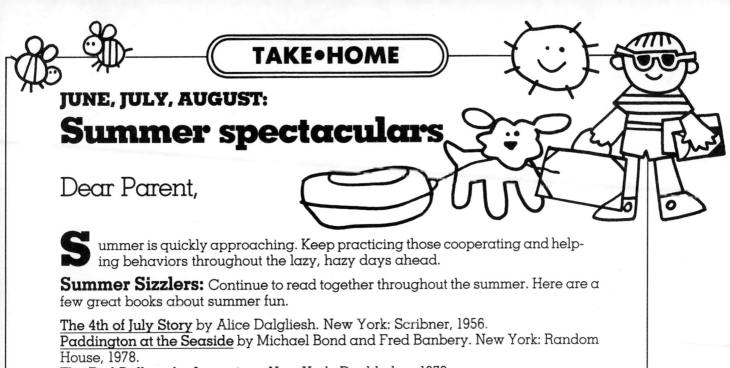

JUNE, JULY, AUGUST:
Summer spectaculars

Dear Parent,

Summer is quickly approaching. Keep practicing those cooperating and help-ing behaviors throughout the lazy, hazy days ahead.

Summer Sizzlers: Continue to read together throughout the summer. Here are a few great books about summer fun.

The 4th of July Story by Alice Dalgliesh. New York: Scribner, 1956.
Paddington at the Seaside by Michael Bond and Fred Banbery. New York: Random House, 1978.
The Red Balloon by Lamorisse. New York: Doubleday, 1978.
Uncle Sam and the Flag by Lee Mountain. Rainbow Books, 1978.
What Can I Do Now, Mommy? by Ginny Graves.

Kid's Koolers: Summer is a great time to make refreshing new drinks for the family. Try some of these delicious concoctions:

1. **Orange Slush:**
1 pint vanilla ice cream, softened
¼ cup frozen orange juice concentrate, thawed

In a blender or small mixing bowl, mix until thick and smooth.

2. **Grape Juice Slush:**
6 oz. frozen grapefruit concentrate
6 oz. frozen orange juice concentrate
6 oz. frozen lemonade concentrate
4 cups water
1 qt. chilled ginger ale

Mix all ingredients except ginger ale. Chill. Just before serving, slowly pour in ginger ale. Serve over crushed ice.

3. **Banana Orange Frosted:**
½ cup orange juice
1 banana
½ cup milk
1 pint orange sherbet

Mix orange juice, milk, banana, and half of the sherbet in the blender on high speed until smooth. Pour into tall glasses. Top each with a scoop of remaining sherbet.

Busy Travelers: If you are going on vacation or taking a day trip in your car, put a pad of paper and some crayons in a bag. Have your child draw pictures of the places you visit. Ask him or her to tell you about each picture, while you write down the child's description. When you get home, put the drawings in order and fasten them together. Your child will enjoy sharing his or her drawings and experiences with family members and friends.

PART IV

Friends with special needs

Mainstreaming handicapped youngsters into regular early childhood programs has increased dramatically during the 1980s. There appear to be, however, three major problems associated with mainstreaming: inadequate facilities, inadequate specialized training for teachers or care givers, and inadequate nonthreatening education of young children about handicaps. In this chapter, we will focus on the third area, the education of young children about handicaps and the development of positive attitudes toward handicapped children.

The children's books, activities, rhyme, and song in this chapter will help to satisfy children's natural curiosity about specific disabilities, familiarize them with the special equipment associated with specific disabilities, and teach them how to help handicapped youngsters feel comfortable in a "real life" school setting. Be a prepared teacher or care giver. Learn as much as you can about blindness, cerebral palsy, and deafness, and teach your class to reach out and love someone different from themselves. Remember, children are only curious and not afraid of physical differences.

Opening the door

BEHAVIORS: Sharing information, cooperating, helping

ACTIVITY: Education on specific handicaps

MATERIALS: children's books about specific handicaps; specialized equipment used for the specific handicaps

DIRECTIONS:

1. Plan a time each month to inform your class about a specific handicap.

2. Read books about the specific handicap. Then discuss the book and answer questions.

3. Obtain specialized equipment from your local rehabilitation institute, hospital, or agency used by people with a specific handicap.

Giving the children an opportunity to examine a wheelchair, crutches, braces, and a scooter might help them understand the specific problems of a handicapped person. It also might help them to be more open to help the handicapped if they get a chance.

Our special visitors

BEHAVIORS: Sharing information, cooperating, helping

ACTIVITY: Listening and questioning

MATERIALS: a professional from your local rehabilitation institute with equipment used by handicapped people

DIRECTIONS: **1.** Invite a special education professional who has worked with young children to your class after your youngsters are familiar with a particular handicap.

2. Ask the professional to talk to the children about the handicap and what they can do to help these people if they are faced with such a situation.

3. Introduce the equipment and, if appropriate, let the children use it—sit in a wheelchair, examine a hearing aid, feel the dots on a braille book.

4. If possible, have the visitor stay for the morning and join the children in their regular routine.

"Kids on the Block"

BEHAVIORS: Cooperating, sharing, rescuing, defending, comforting

ACTIVITY: Puppetry

MATERIALS: professional puppeteers

DIRECTIONS: **1.** Ask your local rehabilitation institute if there is a group of puppeteers who provide skits with "handicapped" puppets who speak, act, and dress like real children. ("Kids on the Block" is the name of a group of puppeteers in Pittsburgh.)

2. If so, invite the group to your school to perform.

3. Make certain the puppeteers offer a question-and-answer session after show.

Our special friends

BEHAVIORS: Cooperating, helping

ACTIVITY: Bulletin board

MATERIALS: Polaroid camera   large block letters   book jackets

DIRECTIONS: **1.** As you complete each special handicap activity throughout the month, take pictures of the children and your special visitors.

2. Place in large block letters at the top of the bulletin board: OUR SPECIAL FRIENDS.

3. Give each child a chance to look at the pictures and place a few on the bulletin board.

4. Place some book jackets from the books you have read on the bulletin board.

CHILDREN'S BOOKS
FOR AND ABOUT HANDICAPS

ALLERGIES

One, Two, Three-Ah-Choo! by Marjorie N. Allen. New York: Coward McCann, 1980.

BLINDNESS

Apartment 3 by Ezra Jack Keats. New York: Macmillan, 1986.
A Cane in Her Hand by Ada Bassett Litchfield. Illus. by Eleanor Mill. Chicago: Albert Whitman, 1977.
The Seeing Stick by Jane Yolan. Illus. by Remy Charlip and Demetra Marslis. New York: Crowell, 1977.

DEAFNESS

Anna's Silent World by Bernard Wolf. Philadelphia: Lippincott, 1974.
A Button in Her Ear by Ada Bassett Litchfield. Illus. by Eleanor Mill. Chicago: Albert Whitman, 1976.
Jamie's Tiger by Jan Wahl. Illus. by Thomas Anthony De Paola. New York: Harcourt Brace Jovanovich, 1978.

HANDICAPS

About Handicaps by Sara Bonnett Stein. Illus. by Dick Frank. New York: Walker, 1974.
Don't Feel Sorry for Paul by Bernard Wolf. Philadelphia: Lippincott, 1974.
He's My Brother by Joseph Leon Lasker. Chicago: Albert Whitman, 1977.
Howie Helps Himself by Joan Fassler. Illus. by Joseph Leon Lasker. Chicago: Albert Whitman, 1975.
Janet at School by Paul White. Illus. by Jeremy Finlay. New York: Crowell, 1978.
Like Me by Alan Brightman. Boston: Little, 1976.
My Brother Steven Is Retarded by Harriet Sobol. New York: Macmillan, 1977.
Rachel by Elizabeth Fanshawe. New York: Dutton, 1975.
Sown in the Boondocks by Wilson Gage. Illus. by Glen H. Rounds. New York: Greenwillow, 1977.

PART V

Friends from around the world

I

n recent years, we have seen an increase in families from different countries in large and small cities throughout the United States. When the children from these families enter early childhood programs, our youngsters are naturally curious about the difference in language, appearance, or both. We need to bridge the gap by studying the cultural and language differences of children in our early childhood class.

Form a Culture Club at your school. Teach the youngsters about faraway places—their customs, their language, and the feelings of those who move far from their homeland. In this section, you'll find children's books, a list of suggestions for fun-to-do activities for your Culture Club, and a rhyme that will broaden your class's world.

Young children will act more prosocially toward different ethnic groups when they understand the concept of individual differences.

Our Culture Club

BEHAVIORS: Cooperating, sharing (information and materials)

DIRECTIONS:

1. Choose one of the ethnic groups represented in your class that kids want to learn more about.

2. Place a large map on the wall. Put a star on the map to show where you live. Put an X on the country you are going to study.

3. Make certain that all of the children know the correct pronunciation of the children's names from that ethnic group.

4. Read books about that particular ethnic group and its culture. Place the book jackets on the walls in the room or on the bulletin board.

5. Ask a language student or teacher from a local high school or college to help you prepare for the rest of this activity.

6. Teach your group several words in the ethnic group's native tongue. Place pictures with the written words below on a bulletin board.

Categorize the words so that they are easier to remember. For example:

NUMBERS   FOOD   ACTION WORDS   FURNITURE

7. Teach the children simple phrases in that language, such as, "My name is _____."

8. Have the children work together to cook a native dish from that country. You may wish to ask one or more of the mothers from that ethnic group to help you and the children.

9. Have parents demonstrate art work or dances from their culture—for example, origami from Japan.

CHILDREN'S BOOKS OF ETHNIC GROUPS IN THE U.S.

CHINESE-AMERICAN

Mr. Fong's Toy Shop by Leo Politi. New York: Macmillan, 1978.

ESKIMOS

Ootah's Lucky Day by Peggy Parish. New York: Harper Junior Books, 1970
On Mother's Lap by Ann Herbert Scott. New York: McGraw-Hill, 1972.

NATIVE AMERICAN

Arrow to the Sun: A Pueblo Indian Tale by Gerald McDermott. New York: Penguin, 1977.

The Drinking Gourd by Ferdinand N. Monjo. New York: Harper Junior Books, 1977.

The Friendly Wolf by Paul Goble and Dorothy Goble. New York: Bradbury Press, 1975.

The Girl Who Loved Wild Horses by Paul Goble. New York: Bradbury Press, 1978.

Granny, the Baby and the Big Gray Thing by Peggy Parish. New York: Macmillan, 1974.

Hawk, I'm Your Brother by Byrd Baylor. New York: Scribner, 1976.

Indian Two Feet and the Wolf Cubs by Margaret Friskey. Chicago: Children's Press, 1971.

Little Runner of the Longhouse by Betty Baker. New York: Harper Junior Books, 1962.

Red Fox and His Canoe by Nathaniel Benchley. New York: Harper Junior Books, 1964.

Small Wolf by Nathaniel Benchley. New York: Harper Junior Books, 1972.

Zeek Silver Moon by Amy Ehrlich. New York: Dial Books for Young Readers, 1972.

CONTINUED

JAPANESE-AMERICANS

Dance, Dance, Amy-Chan! by Lucy Ozone Hawkinson.
Momo's Kitten by Mitsu Yashima and Taro Yashina. New York: Penguin, 1977.

MEXICAN-AMERICANS

Amigo by Byrd Baylor Schweitzer. New York: Macmillan, 1973.
Gilberto and the Wind by Marie Hall Ets. New York: Penguin, 1978.
Nine Days to Christmas by Marie Hall Ets and Aurora Labastida. New York: Viking, 1959.
Song of the Swallows by Leo Politi. New York: Macmillan, 1949.
The Cat in the Hat Dictionary in English and Spanish by Dr. Seuss. New York: Beginner Books, 1967.

CHINESE

When Panda Came to Our House by Helen Zane Jensen. New York: Dial Books for Young Readers, 1985.
Xiao Ming and Katie Visit the Zoo by Zhao Long-yi. Illus. by G. Miller. San Francisco: China Books, 1981.

MULTI CULTURAL

Faces by Barbara Brenner. New York: Dutton, 1970.
My Day Care Book by Nancy and Brand Gladstone. Mt. Rainier, Md.: Gryphon House, 1983.
Why Am I Different? by Norma Simon. Illus. by Dora Leder. Chicago: Albert Whitman, 1976.
Why Are People Different? by Barbara Shook Hazen. Illus. by Kathy Wilburn. New York: Western Publishing, 1985.
What Do I Say? by Norma Simon. Chicago: Albert Whitman, 1967.
What Mary Jo Shared by Janice May Udry. Chicago: Albert Whitman, 1966.
Will I Have a Friend? by Miriam Cohen. New York: Macmillan, 1971.

AFRO-AMERICANS:

Abby by Jeanette Franklin Caines. New York: Harper Junior Books, 1984.

Big Sister Tells Me That I'm Black by Arnold Adoff. New York: Holt, Reinhart & Winston, 1976.

Bobo's Dream by Martha G. Alexander. New York: Dial Books for Young Readers, 1978.

The Case of the Cat's Meow by Crosby Newell Bonsall. New York: Harper Junior Books, 1965.

The Case of the Hungry Stranger by Crosby Newell Bonsall. New York: Harper Junior Books, 1963.

Daddy by Jeanette Franklin Caines. New York: Harper Junior Books, 1977.

Doctor Shawn by Petronella Breinburg. New York: Crowell Junior Books, 1975.

Shawn Goes to School by Petronella Breinburg. New York: Crowell Junior Books, 1975.

Two Is a Team by Lorraine Levy Beim and Beim Jerrold. New York: Harcourt Brace Jovanovich, 1974.

Wagon Wheels by Barbara Brenner. New York: Harper Junior Books, 1984.

Where Wild Willie? by Arnold Adoff. New York: Harper Junior Books, 1978.

Wiley and the Hairy Man by Molly G. Bang. New York: Macmillan, 1976.

A Pocket for Corduroy by Don Freeman. New York: Viking Press, 1978.

Corduroy by Don Freeman. New York: Viking Press, 1968.

Don't Worry Dear by Joan Fassler. New York: Human Sciences Press, 1971.

Dreams by Ezra Jack Keats. New York: Macmillan, 1974.

Evan's Corner by Elizabeth Starr Hill. New York: Holt, 1967.

Everett Anderson's 1, 2, 3 by Lucille B. Clifton. New York: Holt, Reinhart & Winston, 1977.

Goggles by Ezra Jack Keats. New York: Macmillan, 1971.

Hi Cat! by Ezra Jack Keats. New York: Macmillan, 1970.

Horatio by Eleanor Lowenton Clymer. New York: Atheneum, 1974.

I Should Have Stayed in Bed by Joan M. Lexau. New York: Harper Junior Books, 1965.

Jasper and the Hero Business by Betty F. Horvath. New York: Avon, 1978.

Liza Lou and the Yeller Belly Swamp by Mercer Mayer. New York: Macmillan, 1980.

Look at Your Eyes by Paul Showers. New York: Harper Junior Books, 1976.

Louie by Ezra Jack Keats. New York: Greenwillow, 1983.

Me and Nessie by Eloise Greenfield. New York: Crowell Junior Books, 1975.

My Daddy Don't Go to Work by Madeena Spray Nolan. Minneapolis: Carolrhoda Books, 1978.

Peter's Chair by Ezra Jack Keats. New York: Harper Junior Books, 1967.

Pet Show! by Ezra Jack Keats. New York: Macmillan, 1976.

Sam by Ann Herbert Scott. New York: McGraw-Hill, 1967.

CONTINUED

She Come Bringing Me That Little Baby Girl by Eloise Greenfield. New York: Lippincott Junior Books, 1974.

Stevie by John Steptoe. New York: Harper Junior Books, 1976.

The Boy Who Didn't Believe in Spring by Lucille B. Clifton. New York: Dutton, 1978.

The No-Bark Dog by Stan Williamson. Cleveland: Modern Curriculum Press, 1962.

The Snowy Day by Ezra Jack Keats. New York: Viking, 1962.

The Trip by Ezra Jack Keats. New York: Greenwillow, 1978.

What Mary Jo Shared by Janice May Udry. Chicago: Albert Whitman, 1966.

Your Skin and Mine by Paul Showers. New York: Crowell Junior Books, 1965.

Whistle for Willie by Ezra Jack Keats. New York: Penguin, 1977.

The following books are out of print. However, they are all good cultural resources and you may still find them in your public library.

A Time for Flowers by Mark Taylor.

Earth Namer by Margery Bernstein and Janet Kobrin.

Inatuck's Friend by Susan Stark Morrow.

Indian Bunny by Ruth Bernstein.

Meet Miki Takino by Helen Copeland.

Mieko by Leo Politi.

Moy Moy by Leo Politi.

Panda Bear Goes Visiting by Liu Qian.

Soo Ling Finds a Way by June York Behrens.

Three Visitors by Marjorie Hopkins.

Who Am I? by June York Behrens.

PROSOCIAL RESOURCES

"Aggressive and Prosocial Television Programs and the Natural Behavior of Preschool Children." L.K. Friedrich and A.H. Stein. *Monographs of the Society for Research in Child Development*, 1973, 38, serial no. 151.

Altruism and Helping Behavior. J.R. Macaulay and L. Berkowitz (eds.). New York: Academic Press, 1970, 61-73.

"Altruistic Behavior by Children." J.H. Bryan and P. London. *Psychological Bulletin*, 1970, 73, 200-211.

"Children's Cooperation and Helping Behaviors." J.H. Bryan. In E.M. Hetherington (ed.), *Review of Child Development Research*, vol. 5. Chicago: University of Chicago Press, 1975, 127-180.

Children's Friendships. Zick Rubin. Cambridge, Mass.: Harvard University Press, 1980.

"Children's Winning Ways." M. Pines and J. Gottman. *Psychology Today*, 1984, 18, 58-65.

"Developing Comforting Communication Skills in Childhood and Adolescence." B.R. Buleson. *Child Development*, 1982, 53, 1578-1588.

"Dimensions and Correlates of Prosocial Behavior in Young Children." M.R. Yarrow and C.Z. Waxler. *Child Development*, 1976, 47, 118-125.

"Encouraging Helping Behavior." P.F. Marcus and M. Leiserson. *Young Children*, 1978, 33, 24-34.

"Games Children Play." W. Maxwell. *Education Leadership*, 1983, 40, 38-41.

"Growing in Humanness." D.H. Cohen. *Child Today*, 1978, 7, 26.

"Joey Comes to Class." S. Riley. *Early Years*, 1977, 8, 42-43, 55-57.

"Learning Concern for Others." M.R. Yarrow, P.M. Scott, and C.Z. Waxler. *Developmental Psychology*, 1973, 8, 240-260.

"Learning to Care: Developing Prosocial Behavior Among One- and Two-Year-Olds in Group Settings." M.K. Dodge. *Journal of Research and Development in Education*, 1984, 17, 26-30.

Mainstreaming: Ideas for Teaching Young Children. G. Souweine, S. Crimmins, and C. Mazel. Washington, D.C. National Association for the Education of Young Children, 1981.

"Need for Approval, Children's Sharing Behavior, and Reciprocity in Sharing." E. Staub and L. Sherk. *Child Development*, 1971, 42, 805-816.

Promoting the Social Development of Young Children. C.A. Smith. Palo Alto, Calif.: Mayfield, 1982.

"Preaching and Practicing Generosity: Children's Actions and Reactions." J.H. Bryan and N. Tracbek. *Child Development*, 1970, 41, 329-353.

"Prosocial Behavior in Young Children and Parental Guidance." R.L. Mulles. *Child Study Journal*, 1983, 13, 13-21.

CONTINUED

"Prosocial Behavior of Children." D.L. Rosenhan. In S.G. Moore and C.R. Cooper (eds.), *The Young Child: Review of Research*, vol. 3. Washington, D.C.: National Association for the Education of Young Children, 1972, 340-360.

"Prosocial Television and Young Children: The Effects of Verbal Labeling and Role-Playing on Learning and Behavior." L.K. Friedrich and A.H. Stein. *Child Development*, 1975, 46, 27-38.

"Reciprocity and Generosity: Some Determinants of Sharing in Children." M.B. Harris. *Child Development*, 1963, 34, 573-588.

"Research in Review: Prosocial Development in Children." A.S. Honig. *Young Children*, 1982, 37, 51-62.

"Research in Review: Social Cognition: Knowing About Others." S.G. Moore. *Young Children*, 1976, 34, 54-61.

"Social Acceptance: Strategies Children Use and How Teachers Can Help Children Learn Them." N. Hazen, Black, and F. Fleming-Johnson. *Young Children*, 1984, 40, 26-36.

Social and Personality Development. D.R. Shaffer. Monterey, Calif.: Brooks/Cole, 1979.

"Social Interaction and the Development of Social Concepts in Preschool Children." L.I. Nucci and E. Turiel. *Child Development*, 1978, 49, 400-407.

"Social Interaction, Social Competence, and Friendship in Children." J. Gottman, J. Gonso, B. Rasmussen. *Child Development*, 1975, 46, 709-718.

"Social Skill Training of Preschool Children." D.C. Factor and G.L. Schelmoeller. *Child Study Journal*, 1983, 13, 41-56.

"Socialization and the Altruistic Behavior of Children." J.P. Rushton. *Psychological Bulletin*, 1976, 83, 898-913.

"Teaching Children about Individual Differences: Resources for Teaching." M. Shevin-Sapon. *Young Children*, 1983, 38, 24-31.

"Teaching Children to Care." D. Robak. *Children Today*, 1979, 8, 6-7, 34-35.

"The Use of Role-Playing and Induction on Children's Learning of Helping and Sharing Behavior." E. Staub. *Child Development*, 1971, 42, 805-816.

"Training Charity in Children." E. Midlarsky and J.H. Bryan. *Journal of Personality and Social Psychology*, 1967, 5, 408-415.

What's the Difference? Teaching Positive Attitudes Toward People with Disabilities. E. Barnes, C. Berrigan, and D. Beklen. P.O. Box 127, University Station, Syracuse, NY 13210: Human Policy Press, 1978.

Welcome to a prosocial classroom

At _____

children develop positive self images and high self-esteem. Our teachers realize that each child has specific needs, yet all children need to learn prosocial behaviors—getting along with others, developing positive friendships, and becoming part of a group. Understanding, knowledgeable and loving guidance, a supportive and nurturing setting, and opportunities for discovery make this classroom a place where children learn to approach school, daily life, people, and new situations with confidence.

name _____

date _____

TEACHING KIDS TO CARE **159**

"There are only two
lasting bequests
we can hope to give
our children.

One of these is roots;
the other, wings."

—Hodding Carter